"This is a timely book *f*
Christian *offers biblical*
find themselves seeking greater stillness amidst the hysteria of
contemporary life."

– **Pete Greig, 24-7 Prayer**

"Mindfulness is everywhere. For the Christian not quite sure what
to make of it, this book is a real gift, combining theology and
psychology to show how a distinctively Christian mindfulness can
help us become better disciples of Jesus Christ."

– **The Rt Revd Dr Graham Tomlin, The Bishop of Kensington
and President, St Mellitus College**

"This very readable book takes the concepts underlying mindfulness
and opens them up, considering them particularly from a Christian
perspective. Whether you are new to the subject or expanding your
existing knowledge, you will not find a more thorough analysis of
the many issues that this subject brings up."

– **Dr Kate Middleton, psychologist, church leader, and director
of Mind & Soul**

"This book breaks down barriers. To be Christian IS to be mindful –
at least if you are a serious thinker and serious about your faith. To
not be mindful in our faith is to assume, to suppress doubt, to walk
too fast. Mindfulness, the daily practice of being mindful, is therefore
also Christian – it is not the prerogative of another faith or a contract
mindset, as this book clearly explains."

– **Dr Rob Waller, Consultant Psychiatrist in New Zealand and
Director of the Mind and Soul Foundation**

"From my clinical experience, I know that the practice of mindfulness has proved beneficial for many of my clients. I therefore intended to read the book in order to discover more about mindfulness. I confess to being somewhat surprised to find that not only did I learn more, but I found God speaking quite powerfully to me over a personal crisis I was facing in my own life and I found the insights profoundly helpful. I thoroughly recommend this book. The authors have done a superb job in clearly explaining mindfulness and demonstrating how mindfulness is compatible in many ways with Christian prayer and contemplative practice."

– **Heather Churchill, Reg MBACP (senior accredited), Head of Faculty, Waverley Abbey College (CWR)**

Being Mindful, Being Christian

A guide to mindful discipleship

Dr Roger Bretherton
Revd Dr Joanna Collicutt
Dr Jennifer Brickman

MONARCH
BOOKS

Oxford, UK, and Grand Rapids, USA

Published by Monarch Books
an imprint of
Lion Hudson plc
Wilkinson House, Jordan Hill Road,
Oxford OX2 8DR, England
Email: monarch@lionhudson.com
www.lionhudson.com/monarch

ISBN 978 0 85721 729 5
e-ISBN 978 0 85721 786 8

First edition 2016

Acknowledgments
Unless otherwise stated, Scripture quotations taken from the Holy Bible, New International Version Anglicised. Copyright © 1979, 1984, 2011 Biblica, formerly International Bible Society. Used by permission of Hodder & Stoughton Ltd, an Hachette UK company. All rights reserved. "NIV" is a registered trademark of Biblica. UK trademark number 1448790.
Scripture quotations marked NKJV taken from the New King James Version. Copyright © 1982 by Thomas Nelson, Inc. Used by permission. All right reserved.
Scripture quotations marked KJV taken from The Authorized (King James) Version. Rights in the Authorized Version are vested in the Crown. Reproduced by permission of the Crown's patentee, Cambridge University Press.
Scripture quotations marked ESV are from The Holy Bible, English Standard Version® (ESV®) copyright © 2001 by Crossway, a publishing ministry of Good News Publishers. All rights reserved.
Scripture quotations marked NRSV are from The New Revised Standard Version of the Bible copyright © 1989 by the Division of Christian Education of the National Council of Churches in the USA. Used by permission. All Rights Reserved.

A catalogue record for this book is available from the British Library

Printed and bound in the UK, October 2016, LH26

Contents

Acknowledgments

They say it takes a village to raise a child. It also appears to take a village, or at least a small army of people, to produce a book. In our case, this book emerged from a series of conversations, correspondences, and conferences concerning the role of mindfulness in the Christian life. We have no doubt left someone off this list, but in addition to the other contributors to this book, we would like to offer thanks to Richard Adeniran, Brendan Callaghan, Tara Cutland Green, Tim Devine, Richard Johnston, Debbi Malki, Toni Suffolk, and Margaret Whitelaw. We owe the membership of the British Association of Christians in Psychology (BACiP) a debt of gratitude for keeping the conversation on mindfulness energetic and alive. And special thanks particularly are due to Helen Scott, the unflagging administrator of BACiP without whose support very little of this would have been possible. We would also like to thank Jenny Muscat, Drew Stanley, and the team at Monarch for their help and editorial input. Thanks are due also to those who shared their stories and experiences of mindfulness with the contributors. All names are pseudonyms throughout.

Editors

Dr Roger Bretherton is a Clinical Psychologist and Principal Lecturer for Enterprise in the School of Psychology at the University of Lincoln. He has training and years of experience in various psychological therapies that emphasize mindfulness. He is currently chair of BACiP (the British Association of Christians in Psychology) and sits on the board of the Fusion national student network. He speaks regularly in churches and conferences, and works in consultancy with a variety of commercial and public sector organizations. His short book, *The God Lab: 8 Spiritual Experiments You Can Try at Home*, is an experiential guide to the Beatitudes in Matthew's Gospel.

Revd Canon Dr Joanna Collicutt is the Karl Jaspers Lecturer in Psychology and Spirituality at Ripon College, Cuddesdon, a theological college that trains men and women for ministry in the Church of England. She worked for many years as a clinical psychologist in the National Health Service before becoming an academic psychologist of religion. She is the author of several books on the interface between psychology and the Christian faith including *Self-esteem: The Cross and Christian Confidence*; *Meeting Jesus*; *The Dawkins Delusion?*; and *The Psychology of Christian Character Formation*.

Dr Jennifer Brickman is a Chartered Clinical Psychologist. She worked in the NHS for many years as a therapist and supervisor. She now works in private practice providing psychological support to Christians in ministry. She and her husband Mark, an Associate Minister at St Aldates Church in Oxford, have developed The Encounter Course. This integrates insights from mindfulness, compassion research, and cognitive therapy with biblical narratives to help participants grow in emotional and spiritual health.

Contributors

Dr Tanya Arroba
Chartered Occupational Psychologist and Visiting Fellow at Cranfield University School of Management.
Chapter: *The Mindful Organization*

Dr Roger Bretherton
Chartered Clinical Psychologist and Principal Lecturer in the University of Lincoln School of Psychology.
Chapters: *What's All the Fuss About?; Mindful Bible Reading; Mindfulness and Christian Character; Mindful Gratitude; Mindful Wisdom; The Mindful Organization*

Dr Jennifer Brickman
Chartered Clinical Psychologist.
Chapters: *The Mindful Person; Turning to the Compassionate God; Turning Inward with Eyes to See*

Revd Canon Dr Joanna Collicutt
Karl Jaspers Lecturer in Psychology of Religion and Spirituality at Ripon College, Cuddesdon and Fellow in Psychology of Religion at Harris Manchester College, Oxford.
Chapters: *The Mindful God; The Mindful Person; The Mindful Christian; Turning Inwards with Eyes to See; Mindful Bible Reading*

Revd Dr Araminta Hull
Clinical Psychologist, Anglican Priest, and Advisor on Spiritual Direction.
Chapter: *Mindful Reflection*

Dr Nimmi Hutnik
Chartered Counselling Psychologist and Associate Professor at London South Bank University School of Health and Social Care.
Chapter: *The Mindful Person*

Revd Shaun Lambert
Minister at Stanmore Baptist Church, Mindfulness Scholar, and Accredited Psychotherapist.
Chapter: *Turning Towards Pain and Need*

Dr Claire Roberts
Chartered Clinical Psychologist and Pain Specialist.
Chapters: *Turning Inward with Eyes to See; Turning Towards Pain and Need*

Professor Michael Wang
Emeritus Professor of Clinical Psychology and former DClinPsy Course Director at the University of Leicester.
Chapter: *The Mindful Person*

Dr Bonnie Poon Zahl
Academic Specializing in Psychology of Religion, University of Oxford.
Chapter: *Turning to the Compassionate God*

Mindfulness: What's All the Fuss About?

Mindfulness is everywhere

Wherever I go, people are talking about mindfulness.

Mindfulness is big. Hardly a day goes by without a newspaper or a TV programme or a Twitter account expounding the virtues of practising mindfulness. And it's in every sphere of our culture. There is almost no domain of Western society where mindfulness hasn't been recommended as a beneficial practice. We hear it being recommended for well-being in the workplace. It will reduce stress, increase concentration, promote work engagement, and improve relationships with colleagues. Many workplaces now offer formal training in mindfulness and may even have a regular mindfulness group for employees.

It's also in vogue in the health sector. Go to your doctor feeling depressed, or anxious, suffering from chronic pain, or feeling burned out and it's pretty likely that at some point you'll find yourself face-to-face with a highly trained healthcare professional recommending a mindfulness programme to you. Similarly in schools and education, mindfulness is being taught to young people as a beneficial aid to their ability to study. Not only does it allow them to concentrate more effectively, but it also improves their psychological well-being.

Mindfulness is everywhere. Just a quick tally of mindfulness titles in the well-being section of your local bookshop will no doubt confirm this. The practice has caught the popular imagination through the endorsement of well-informed celebrity advocates such as Oprah Winfrey and Ruby Wax. Its vast appeal is illustrated by the growth of the mindfulness app and associated website, Headspace. Co-founded in 2010 by former Buddhist monk and circus performer, Andy Puddicombe, the Headspace app was launched in 2012, and by 2015 claimed to have over 2 million users.

Indeed, so pervasive is the influence of mindfulness that the UK government set up the Mindfulness All-Party Parliamentary Group (MAPPG)[1] to review the benefits of the practice for the nation as a whole. The ensuing report, entitled "Mindful Nation UK", originally published in October 2015, reviewed research spanning many of the spheres mentioned above – health, education, workplace, and the criminal justice system. Having consulted numerous leading researchers, practitioners, and beneficiaries, the group concluded that the widespread teaching of mindfulness was imperative for the future well-being of UK citizens. The final chapter of the report considers the prodigious challenge of making mindfulness available more widely and offers recommendations for funding and training additional mindfulness teachers. For example, the report recommends that by 2020 the National Health Service should have trained an additional 1,200 mindfulness teachers so as to increase its availability to those who suffer with recurrent depression each year.

It's not just a fad or a popular movement. Behind the recommendations of the MAPPG report lies an equally vast scientific literature establishing the psychological benefits of mindfulness. Studies have linked regular mindfulness meditation with decreases in anxiety, depression, and irritability.[2,3]

Meditators show improvement in reaction time, and increased mental and physical stamina. The quality of relationships reportedly improves for those who meditate, as does immune system functioning – mindfulness helps people fight off colds, flu, and other diseases. Even the impact of the most challenging health conditions of our age, like stress-induced hypertension, chronic pain, cancer, and substance abuse, can be reduced through mindful practice.[4]

And this is just the tip of the iceberg. The amount of scientific research currently directed towards mindfulness is overwhelming. One review suggested that since the turn of the millennium, academic research on mindfulness has increased twentyfold. At present, roughly 500 scientific papers on the subject are published each year. Admittedly, not everybody is so impressed with these findings, and some have even suggested that the benefits of mindfulness as a universal good are an exaggeration.[5] But by virtue of the sheer volume of publication, there are only a handful of people on the planet currently able to keep abreast of the explosive growth of mindfulness science.

What we mean by mindfulness

So mindfulness is big. But what is it? It may help to spell out what we mean by mindfulness.

Perhaps unsurprisingly there isn't one easy cover-it-all definition of mindfulness. Numerous definitions are available, and different practitioners tend to emphasize different elements of the practice, according to their preference.

Most psychologists like to begin with the definition provided by Jon Kabat-Zinn. As the principal developer of Mindfulness-Based Stress Reduction (MBSR), Kabat-Zinn is often considered the instigator of the current vogue of mindfulness.

Although he was trained in mindfulness by Thich Nhat Hanh, a Vietnamese Buddhist monk, he was the first to place mindfulness in a scientific context, eventually de-emphasizing its roots in Buddhism. He founded the Stress Reduction Clinic at the University of Massachusetts Medical School in 1979. It was there that he developed his eight-session mindfulness programme, demonstrating the evidence of its effectiveness in treating a range of health conditions including psoriasis, pain, anxiety, and immune function.

Kabat-Zinn gained increasing recognition with the publication of his first book, *Full Catastrophe Living*,[6] in 1991. His second book, *Wherever You Go, There You are*, became an international bestseller. It was here that he offered his often-quoted definition: "mindfulness means paying attention in a particular way: on purpose, in the present moment, and non-judgementally".[7] A few short words that capture the mindful state and the key ingredients of its practice.

There are other definitions though. In 2004 a gathering of international experts in the field reviewed the range of definitions that had been offered up until that time, with the aim of producing an agreed understanding of what mindfulness entailed. Ultimately they settled on a two-part understanding. Mindfulness, they agreed, involves a *what* and a *how*. It requires (a) the self-regulation of attention, and (b) an attitude of curiosity, openness, and acceptance.[8]

Some people of course are quite strict in the way they use the terminology of mindfulness. For example, some would draw a very clear line between the terms "mindfulness" and "meditation". Other practitioners however seem to ignore this distinction, they use the words mindfulness and meditation interchangeably as if they are the same thing, and it's not uncommon to find writers on the subject putting both words together and referring to mindfulness meditation, even when the exercises they outline would be categorized as one or the other by some.

A further distinction that is often drawn in the mindfulness literature lies between mindful practice and mindfulness. In certain respects this is similar to the differentiation sometimes made by Christians between praying and prayerfulness. Praying, according to this view, is the clearly identifiable activity in which we make time to connect or communicate with God; prayerfulness, on the other hand, may represent the slightly looser and indefinable way in which we live our lives in perpetual and constant communication with God, without this attitude necessarily being evident to an external observer. Prayer is an activity, prayerfulness is an attitude.

The same distinction is often drawn with mindfulness. Formal Mindful practice is the time explicitly set aside from other distractions to practise mindful exercises such as attending to breath or observing thoughts. Mindfulness on the other hand is often viewed as the use of the mindful attitude in the various activities of everyday life, sometimes called mindfulness on-the-go. It includes mindful walking, mindful eating, mindful cooking, mindful drawing, mindful door-opening... In fact, pretty much any daily activity can be performed mindfully, and that is what everyday mindfulness refers to.

In this book we've inclined towards a broad understanding of mindfulness. We use the words "mindful" and "mindfulness" to refer to both formal and informal practices, observable behaviours and a deeper, more hidden attitude. In so doing, we run the risk of irritating those who would prefer a more technical approach to the subject. But for the purposes of this book we believe that the definition should be easy to remember, capture the essence of mindfulness, and do justice to the breadth and complexity of our subject without tying it down too tightly.

Over the chapters that follow we look at the application of mindfulness to various aspects of Christian living. These aspects are pretty diverse. We look at hospitality, focusing attention on thoughts, the body, and our circumstances. We note how mindfulness can help us be compassionate, grateful, and wise. The applications are different, but the approach is the same. Whatever the specifics of the application, mindfulness, in the way we use the term, means *paying attention to the present moment without wishing it were otherwise.*

Is mindfulness OK for Christians?

Mindfulness is everywhere. The scientific evidence is stacking up in its favour. Mindfulness is good. What possible objection could anyone make to the enthusiastic promotion of mindful practice in all domains of life?

A lot of Christians however are worried or confused by the burgeoning field of mindfulness. They don't quite know what to make of it. As Christians and psychologists, it's not unusual for us to be approached by people in church asking what we think of mindfulness. Some people, at work or for health reasons, have been referred for mindfulness training and want some trustworthy guidance before signing up. Others approach us covertly, almost guiltily, to confess that they practise mindfulness and find it helpful, but aren't quite sure how it squares with their Christian faith. In one way or another, both groups of people are asking the same question: is mindfulness OK for Christians?

If you're asking that question, we wrote this book for you.

One of the reasons some Christians are uneasy about the recent rise of mindfulness in public awareness is the perception that it offers a competing spiritual path to Christianity. From this perspective the modern surge in mindfulness could be considered misleading. Under the guise of promoting an entirely secular approach to well-being, harmony, and peace in the world, the spread of mindfulness could be insidiously encouraging an entire generation to embrace Far Eastern philosophy and spirituality.

In the chapters that follow, we hope to demonstrate that mindful awareness, far from being the exclusive possession of any particular religion or ideology, is a universal quality of attention, available to all human beings. There is of course a rich Christian tradition of mindful spiritual practices, stretching back over the last 2,000 years, to which we will refer frequently. But ultimately being mindful is neither Christian nor Buddhist nor secular, it is a state of mind accessible and relevant to all of us. In fact you probably adopt something very much like a mindful state when you engage in various activities of the Christian life. When you pray or worship, when you read Scripture or listen to a sermon, when you search for wisdom or seek guidance from God, the likelihood is that you are being mindful. Directing your attention and opening your mind. As you read, we gently invite you to consider where being mindful may be helpful in following Jesus.

Other Christians are wary of mindfulness because of the belief that it somehow requires us to empty our minds. This is often linked to the concern that mindfulness meditation will open us up to malign spiritual influence, that emptying ourselves will allow malignant forces to flood in. However, it is probably already evident from the definitions surveyed above that mindfulness is not about emptying the mind but rather about observing it. Some Christian writers have rewritten the word as mind-fullness, to emphasize the fact that the practice involves directing our attention like a spotlight towards certain processes, like breathing or walking, cooking or reading. Far from being empty, the mind is filled with whatever it attends to, and in some cases this will be a full awareness of God.

What this book is about

This book arose out of a series of conferences organized by the British Association of Christians in Psychology (BACiP). We have over 200 UK psychologists on our books and over several years we gathered together to discuss the various dilemmas and controversies that the recent popularity of mindfulness poses for Christians. It was an intense period of conversation and debate, not just at the conferences, but in online discussion forums too. We addressed many of the issues involved in being mindful and being Christian. We didn't always agree – and still sometimes don't. But after four consecutive conferences talking it over, we decided we needed to put some of the expertise gathered all in one place. And that's what this book is about.

You will no doubt gather from the list of contributors that there are ten of us. That list tells you who we are and which bits we wrote. We are all psychologists or friends of BACiP who gave something somehow at some point to that series of conferences. The list includes leading experts in Clinical Psychology, Counselling Psychology, Occupational Psychology, Neuropsychology, and Psychology of Religion. We count among our number several well-published academics, and a handful of ordained clergy. As a group we have clocked hundreds of thousands of hours of experience in using psychology to help individuals and groups in all kinds of contexts – often working with churches. We have all practised and taught mindfulness to some extent. We bring a diverse range of expertise to bear on the subject. But, rather than linking together a set of disjointed chapters we've tried to write with one voice. When we tell stories from our own experience sometimes we use "we" and sometimes we use "I". In different chapters, the "I" is a different person, but the "we" speaks for all of us.

The book is therefore divided into two parts: "Being Mindful" and "Being Christian". In the first part we tell you what mindfulness is. We lay the groundwork to understand the nature of mindfulness. We look at it theologically (as originating in the mindfulness of God), psychologically (as a state of mind, body, and brain), and biblically (as evident in the teaching of Jesus). The second part (Being Christian) is practical. We take a look at various ways in which a mindful approach to Christian living can be enormously helpful. We have divided this section into four Cs:

- **Compassion:** in which we look at how mindfulness can help us connect or reconnect with the compassionate heart of a loving God.

- **Courage:** where we examine the way a mindful attitude can help us turn towards those things we would rather avoid in ourselves and in the world around us.

- **Curiosity:** allowing mindfulness to assist our reading of the Bible and our moments of reflection on God.

- **Character:** the application of mindfulness to character formation, gratitude, wisdom, and the life of modern organizations.

The second part of the book is designed to leave you free to skip around to what interests you most. Scattered throughout the chapters are text boxes designed to help you get a deeper understanding of the issues covered. We've given them frivolous titles just to keep you on your toes. Not every chapter has all six boxes, but here's what we've called them and what they contain:

- **Yes ... but ...**: answers to common concerns that Christians express about mindfulness.

- **Where Did it Come From?**: historical summaries of different places and times when Christians have developed approaches similar to mindfulness.

- **Get Some Exercise!**: exercises and practices that allow you to try the content of each chapter for yourself.

- **Help ... I'm a Geek**: a handful of references (books, articles, websites) that act as a starting point if you feel the need to research further.

- **By the Book**: in-depth Bible exegesis on passages pertinent to key aspects of mindful awareness.

- **When Two or Three are Gathered**: questions for group discussion for those who read the book as part of a book club or a home group.

Each of them offers you the chance to interact with the content of the book in a different way. You can choose which ones most interest you as you make your way through the chapters that follow. To kick things off we have included a *Help... I'm a Geek* box in this section. There has been a flurry of writing about mindfulness from a Christian perspective recently and the various books and resources cited here address the practice from different perspectives. If you are serious about the place of mindful awareness in the Christian life, they are certainly worth looking at.

Help... I'm a Geek

Other sources on mindfulness

Shaun Lambert has spent over a decade researching mindfulness and is currently completing a doctoral thesis on the Christian theology of mindful practice. He has written several books on the subject, and has elaborated the theological and practical background here:

Lambert, S. (2016). *Putting on the Wakeful One: Attuning to the Spirit of Jesus Through Watchfulness*. Watford: Instant Apostle.

Tim Stead has worked with arguably the leading UK expert in mindfulness, Professor Mark Williams at the University of Oxford, and has written an elegant view of how mindful practice fits with Christian spirituality:

Stead, T. (2016). *Mindfulness and Christian Spirituality: Making Space for God*. London: SPCK.

Brian Draper brings his characteristically profound and prophetic voice to the subject of mindfulness. Accepting its benefits, but arguing for something deeper than an individualistic consumerist practice:

Draper, B. (2016). *Soulfulness: Deepening the Mindful Life*. London: Hodder & Stoughton.

Sally Welch cuts to the chase with a short book of mindful practices for Christians. If you prefer to learn about mindful Christianity by doing it, this is a great place to start:

Welch, S. (2016). *How to Be a Mindful Christian: 40 Simple Spiritual Practices*. Norwich: Canterbury Press.

For several years now Richard Johnston has developed a distinctively Christian approach to mindful practice, which he calls Christian Mindfulness. He has produced an extensive range of resources, meditations, training programmes, and writings which can all be accessed at his website: www.christianmindfulness.co.uk

A complete list of sources is provided in the reference section at the end of the book.

An invitation to mindful discipleship

If this book does what we hope it will do, then by the end of it you will not only know what mindfulness is, but also where you can apply it in your daily following of Christ.

When I was first formally trained in mindfulness several decades ago, I was surprised by what I learned. It dawned on me that a state of mind, a quality of awareness, that I had been practising ever since I was a child, had another name. Formerly I had called it relaxing with God, or being in the moment, or soaking in the Spirit, or resting in Jesus. Latterly I learned that it was called mindfulness. It was also much more than that, but being mindful was certainly the attitude of openness and willingness to dwell in the present that underlay many of my most precious experiences of God. Mindfulness was not entirely foreign, if anything it was all too familiar.

We are therefore not calling you to become an unthinking advocate of mindfulness, but rather offering an invitation to consider where a mindful attitude may help you follow Jesus more closely. It's an invitation to explore a path of mindful discipleship.

But all paths by definition have to begin somewhere. So where do we begin? We begin, where all discipleship begins… with God.

Being Mindful

The Mindful God

In the beginning

Before human beings discovered mindfulness, God was mindful.

The mindfulness of God is attentive and watchful; it is open and hospitable to what it encounters, rather than defensive and reactive; it describes without rushing to judgment. In many ways it is very like human mindfulness. But it is also profoundly different. After all we're talking about *God* here: "For My thoughts are not your thoughts, nor are your ways My ways, says the Lord. For as the heavens are higher than the earth, so are My ways higher than your ways, and My thoughts than your thoughts" (Isaiah 55:8–9 NKJV).

God's mindfulness comes before all human attempts at mindfulness (just as his love and forgiveness come before all human attempts at love and forgiveness). It is *first*: through it all mindful creatures were brought into being. It is fundamentally creative and re-creative. Healthy human mindfulness is a participation in this creative and re-creative mindfulness of God. The world could not have been brought into being without the mindfulness of God, and it could not continue to be sustained without the mindfulness of God.

God thinks therefore I am

The Old Testament links the mindfulness of God to his loving care of human beings. The psalmist asks "What is man that you are mindful of him, and the son of man that you care for him?" (Psalm 8:4 ESV). On the face of it this verse seems to be posing the question of why God would bother with puny little creatures like us, but some scholars have seen something deeper here. They suggest that the psalmist is instead pondering what it means to be human – "what is man?", and he comes to the answer "that you are mindful of him". That is, we are human precisely because God is mindful of us! If God were to stop keeping us in mind we would cease to be. God's mindfulness is what gives us our souls.

Where Did it Come From?

Hebrew and Greek

In the Hebrew Old Testament the word for "be mindful" is zākar and in the Greek version of the Old Testament (which dates from the third century BC) the word is mimnēskomai – the same word used by the thief on the cross in the Greek New Testament.

In the Old Testament God's mindfulness is not just psychological; it is "ontological". This means that when God is mindful things come into existence and when he ceases to be mindful of something it ceases to exist.

Hebrew poetry often uses "parallelisms", which means that it says the same thing twice but using different words. This helps us to work out what the words mean. In the case of Psalm 8 we find the parallelism "What is man that you are mindful of him, and the son of man that you care for him?" This tells us that being mindful means something very like "caring for". The "care for" word is pāqad, which can mean "visit", and so it has overtones of hospitality, something that is also characteristic of human mindfulness.

Elsewhere in the psalms, God's constant non-judgmental scrutiny is linked with the very act of forming the psalmist as a developing foetus: "My frame was not hidden from you when I was made in the secret place, when I was woven together in the depths of the earth. Your eyes saw my unformed body; all the days ordained for me were written in your book before one of them came to be" (Psalm 139:15–16).

Yes... but...

Is it right to use the word "mindful" to describe God?

The Jews had their own understanding of mindfulness before Buddhism developed its version. There are similarities and differences between them.

In Judaism mindfulness is primarily a divine attribute, closely related to God's loving-kindness (ḥesed), but one that human beings can emulate. In addition to being contemplative it is also active; this more active aspect of mindfulness corresponds well to a psychological state called "flow".

The mindfulness of Christ reflects the mindfulness of the God of the Old Testament. So, while Christian understandings of mindfulness are later than Buddhism, their origin in Judaism is older. And of course Christian mindfulness is older than modern psychotherapy. There is a sense in which "we had it first", and we need to be confident about acknowledging this.

The Hebrew word that is translated "mindful" in English Bibles has a range of meanings that include "remember", "keep in mind", "call to mind", "be concerned about", and – interestingly – "meditate". It describes a kind of loving attentiveness, a calling to consciousness – as when we remember a friend's birthday and communicate our remembering by sending a card. It's what we mean when we say to someone who is going through a difficult time, "I'll be thinking of you".

God asserts that his basic nature is to be mindful of his people: "Can a mother forget the baby at her breast and have no compassion on the child she has borne? Though she may forget, I will not forget you! See, I have engraved you on the palms of my hands" (Isaiah 49:15–16a). Jesus himself describes this divine mindfulness in one of his parables: all the time the prodigal son was away in a far country his father was mindful of him.

The hospitable God

When the watchful and attentive father of the prodigal is finally reunited with his son he runs with open arms to greet him and hosts a great party. This is a picture of the hospitable God of Psalm 23 who not only feeds and guides the psalmist, but also lays a table for him and anoints him as an honoured guest. Psalm 23 ends with a statement of trust in God's goodness and "loving-kindness". It sums up God's starting attitude to human beings – an attitude of love that treats us as if he is pleased with us even when we don't look very worthy of this approval. It shows itself in compassionate action – an opening of the arms and the heart that makes you vulnerable to being hurt, abused, and rejected. Reflecting with wonder on this attribute of God, Paul writes: "God demonstrates his own love for us in this: While we were still sinners, Christ died for us" (Romans 5:8).

Hospitality, openness, and refraining from judging are key aspects of human mindfulness. The practitioner is encouraged to take a hospitable attitude to whatever thoughts and experiences arise, to consider them as they are, without evaluating them or getting bogged down in analysing them. Just as the father of the prodigal resists the urging of his older son to judge, the practitioner of mindfulness aims to resist the habit of evaluating. Of course there are times and places for judging and evaluating, but what is distinctive about mindfulness, and extraordinary about God, is that judgment is suspended for a while.

Jesus often talks about this suspension of judgment in terms of seed time and harvest. At the end of time the productivity of the fig tree will be evaluated, but for now we should "Leave it alone" (Luke 13:8); the wheat will be separated from the weeds but until then "let both grow together" (Matthew 13:30). We have to resist our human tendency to knee-jerk reactions and the rush to judgment because this is not God's way. Jesus taught that right up until the one and final judgment God gives the benefit of the doubt.

"Jesus, remember me"

Jesus didn't only teach this; he showed it in his acceptance of a dying thief who turned to him at the end of a life of crime (Luke 23:42). We are inclined to be cynical about "deathbed conversions"; they seem to be too easy – a way of getting the benefits of heaven even after a lifetime's sinning. Yet somehow God sees it differently. Indeed, this is one way in which "my thoughts are not your thoughts". Jesus saw something in the man who hung beside him, perhaps something missed by others. Whatever it was, it was enough for Jesus to give him the benefit of the doubt and to invite him into paradise.

By the Book

"Be opened"

The whole of this chapter focuses on the Bible, but if you are eager for more take a look at Mark 7:24–37.

This is the account of the meeting between Jesus and a foreign woman on foreign soil. At first Jesus does not seem inclined to offer this woman the hospitality of his table, appearing to judge her on the basis of her ethnicity. But in response to her words he sets this first instinct aside and is able to see her simply as herself without any further evaluation. Jesus' mindfulness of the woman is depicted as a kind of opening up.

It is significant that he goes on from this to heal another foreigner, this time a deaf man, with the words "Ephphatha" – "be **opened**". As Jesus touches this man in a deeply intimate way it's as if he is passing his own recent opening up on to him.

To be healed by Jesus is to be opened – to become hospitable like Jesus. This is an insight we can bring to reading the Bible. To read the Bible mindfully is to read it with an openness to the healing presence of Jesus

The thief asks Jesus to "remember" him in that same word that is translated "be mindful of" in Psalm 8. We can see from this that the thief is asking Jesus to do more than keep him on the radar. He's asking for mindfulness – for loving, hospitable attention. And he gets it. Just as in Psalm 8, something creative is going on: it is through Jesus' mindfulness that this individual turns from thief into human person. Jesus' mindfulness gives him his soul. The broken pieces of his life are gathered up and he is made whole – literally "re-membered".

We might be tempted to think that what saved the thief on the cross was his insight into his sins and his decision to turn to Christ. We might be tempted to think that what saved the prodigal son was his insight into his sins and his decision to go home to his father. In a way we would be right to think this because our faith does save us, as Jesus told people again and again. Yet something more fundamental is at work: *the grace of God.*

Ephesians 2:8 sums this up well by saying that we have been saved through (our) faith but *by* (God's) grace. Our faith is the way we express a gut instinct that God may do us good and be prepared to open wide his arms to us even when we don't deserve it. It's based on a hope that God is after all still mindful of us even when we repeatedly forget him. So, while the thief and the prodigal son needed to make a decision to turn homewards, what ultimately saved them was the watchful attention and unconditional welcome that had all the time been there for them.

The mind of Christ

"Let the same mind be in you that was in Christ Jesus," writes Paul in his letter to the Philippians (Philippians 2:5 NRSV). What does he mean? How might we have the mind of Christ? What Paul writes next is fascinating, for it is all about sitting lightly and letting go – the stuff of mindfulness practice. Perhaps, then, we are to have the "mindfulness of Christ"?

Paul writes that Jesus is equal with God but that he did not grasp this equality tightly or use it for his own ends. Instead he laid it aside and emptied himself so that he could undertake his mission. The crucial thing to understand here is that Paul is not saying that Christ emptied his mind (he clearly didn't!), but that he emptied himself of things that would get in the way of his relationship with his heavenly Father.

One place that we see him doing this is in the wilderness. Jesus is tempted by Satan to meet his personal needs for food, for wealth and power, and to exploit his special relationship with his Father. He systematically refuses to do this by emptying himself of the "what's in it for me?" agenda. This is worked out in his insistence that his mission is to serve rather than be served (Matthew 20:28). Paul describes this as "taking the very nature of a servant" (Philippians 2:7). A psychologist might describe it as "quieting the ego".

Later in the garden of Gethsemane Jesus does this again. His ego wants one thing; his Father's will is different. Somehow he manages to quiet his ego, to let go of his concerns, and to move from a place of deep struggle to a place of peace, ready to walk the way of the cross. Or, as Paul describes it, "he humbled himself by becoming obedient to death – even death on a cross" (Philippians 2:8). This is the mind of Christ that Paul exhorts his readers to share.

Help... I'm a Geek

Further reading in this area

For a short but deep book about the waiting and watching of God as it is worked out in Christ's passion see:

Vanstone, W. (1982). *The Stature of Waiting*. London: Darton, Longman & Todd.

For a helpful summary of what it means for God to remember (or be mindful of) see chapter 8 "Memory and the divine embrace" from:

Swinton, J. (2012). *Dementia: Living in the Memories of God*. London: SCM.

If you want to find out more about the active side of mindfulness:

Csikszentmihalyi, M. (1990). *Flow: The Psychology of Optimal Experience*. New York: Harper & Row.

For more on the father who watches for the prodigal son see chapter 6 "The meeting" from:

Duff, J. & Collicutt, J. (2006). *Meeting Jesus: Human Responses to a Yearning God*. London: SPCK.

An academic treatment of the way that memory is treated in the Old Testament can be found in a classic text:

Childs, B. (1962). *Memory and Tradition in Israel*. London: SCM.

A classic book on contemporary prayer that places a particular emphasis on prayer as a kind of open hospitality to God (mirroring God's hospitality to us):

Keating, T. (1986). *Open Mind, Open Heart*. London: Continuum. Many versions available.

A complete list of sources is provided in the reference section at the end of the book.

Of course, Jesus had already said something very similar: "'Whoever wants to be my disciple must deny themselves and take up their cross daily and follow me. For whoever wants to save their life will lose it, but whoever loses their life for me will save it. What good is it for someone to gain the whole world, and yet lose or forfeit their very self?'" (Luke 9:23–25). Jesus isn't talking about emptying of the mind but of quieting the ego and letting go of those everyday "what if?" thoughts that so often seem to overwhelm us and divert us from "seeking the kingdom" (Matthew 6:31–33). These thoughts arise from our tendency to grasp greedily, or more often anxiously, at relationships, wealth, pleasure, and possessions. Our bad habits in these areas can so easily turn into addictions.

To have the mind of Christ is to sit lightly in relation to all of these things, to be prepared to set them aside so that we can be properly mindful of him, as he is of us. In this way we will, like the prodigal son and the thief on the cross, find that our true self has been re-membered – that we have been saved.

"Since, then, you have been raised with Christ... set your minds on things above"

God's mindfulness is behind the creation of the cosmos. In Genesis 1 we read that his creative attention brought things into being, and that creation was also punctuated by periods of contemplation on God's part, as he saw that what he had made was good. Finally, on the seventh day God rested (Genesis 2:2) – not the rest of fatigue but something more like satisfaction at a job well done and a time simply to be in the present. We are told that God blessed this way of being (Genesis 2:3). So, God's creative mindfulness and his contemplative mindfulness are both behind our creation.

But God's mindfulness also has its part to play in our salvation. We've seen that one way of thinking about this is as being remembered and made whole. Another way that the Bible talks about this is as being *raised*. When we know that God holds us in mind we begin to be raised to our full stature. We see this very clearly in the story of Zacchaeus (Luke 19:2–10) who, we are told, was a small man who climbed up a tree in order to "see who Jesus was" but instead was *seen by* Jesus. Jesus was mindful of Zacchaeus; as a result Zacchaeus' life changed dramatically. In a crucial detail we are told that Zacchaeus "stood up" – literally "made a stand" (verse 8). Somehow being held in mind by Jesus raised him up.

Some years ago I experienced something similar. I had gone to give a church talk, which was to be followed by afternoon tea. When I had finished speaking a rather eccentric-looking gentleman from the audience approached me and said he had some points of detail arising from the talk that he'd like to discuss further with me. My host quickly and quietly moved me away, whispering in my ear that it was probably best not to get into conversation with this person, and rolling his eyes as he did so.

But, as is often the case, the gentleman in question was not to be put off so easily and managed to get a seat opposite me at tea. I could not escape, so I made the best of it. I decided to listen to what he had to say. This required a good deal of attention because he rambled quite a lot; nevertheless I could detect thoughtfulness and knowledge behind his questions, and I engaged properly with them. We were talking for about five minutes, and I found myself wondering if this was boring everyone else at the table or upsetting my host. Then the gentleman stood up, gave a little bow, and went on his way. My host then said, "Can I ask you a question?" I thought he too was going to quiz me about my talk. Instead he asked, "Could you really understand Mr X? It sounded as if you were taking him seriously. To my regret, I've never managed to do that." I explained that I was used to talking to a wide range of people because of my work in clinical psychology, but also that the gentleman had been attempting to make some intelligent points. Another person at the table then said something that I have never forgotten: "Doesn't Mr X normally walk with a stoop? – yet he just walked out of here standing up straight."

What was going on? Essentially, I as a naive visitor did not have a history with this individual and I wasn't inclined to judge him on the basis of what others told me; I suspended the tendency to evaluate, and just let him be. For a while I simply gave him my undivided attention; I was mindful of him. Somehow my holding him properly in mind enabled him to stand tall and be more fully the human being that God had in mind. In a very small way, and for a very limited time, we had all participated in the mindfulness of God.

When Two or Three are Gathered...

Questions for group discussion

You may like to use the following questions to discuss the mindfulness of God as a small group.

How does the loving, attentive gaze of God (for example as described in Psalm 139) make us feel – secure, peaceful, ashamed, anxious?

If we exist because God holds us in mind, what does this imply about what happens when we die?

If we are given our humanity by God's mindfulness does that have any implications for our attitudes to other people, especially those who have physical or mental impairments?

Is there a difference between holding someone in mind and praying for them?

The Mindful Person

Anyone who has practised mindfulness knows that the mindful state is not just about the mind. It's not all in our heads. When we are mindful, we don't disappear into our thoughts. If anything, we become more aware of the world around us – and of our thoughts too, for that matter. For this reason mindfulness has sometimes been thought of as three separate components:[1] as an *intention* (the values of non-judgment that lie behind the practice), as *attention* (the focus of awareness in the here and now), and as an *attitude* (the kindness with which we direct our attention).

Yes... but...

Won't mindfulness make us spiritually vulnerable?

An altered state of consciousness (ASC) is any condition which is significantly different from a normal waking state. Some Christians are very concerned by ASCs. They worry that such states render us vulnerable to malign spiritual forces. Many church groups and organizations advise their members against hypnosis because of these concerns. Some argue that mindfulness involves elements of self-hypnosis and is therefore to be shunned by Christians.

But ASCs are a normal part of living, and therefore Christians experience them without concern all the time. Meditative prayer can be classed as an ASC. Daydreaming is an ASC. All of us pass through ASCs when we fall asleep and when we wake up.

Superstitious Christians in the Middle Ages believed that a sneeze created a momentary ASC and that people had to be protected from demonic attack by a blessing – hence the traditional "bless you" response to a spontaneous sneeze. In a similar vein, some "Deliverance Ministries" believe that traumatic incidents such as car crashes (which produce the ASC of shock) can result in demon possession.

There is however a big difference between actively seeking satanic influence (e.g. taking part in séances or Ouija board sessions) and ASCs in which no such act of will is involved. Are these doctrines really scriptural and theologically justified? Did Jesus really die on the cross to save us and win the victory over Satan only to have his followers spend their lives running in fear from everyday human psychological states? If we have the most powerful force in the universe within us, is it really credible that we should so easily fall prey to the forces of darkness that have been overcome by Christ's victory on the cross?

In this chapter we've tried to keep it simple. We look at all these components of mindfulness from several different angles. Firstly we look at what it is like to be mindful – from the inside: what the mind is doing in mindful practice. We then turn to the body. Many forms of mindful practice involve becoming adept at noticing bodily changes in breath, sensation, and movement. We look at how mindfulness interacts with and benefits the body. And thirdly, we turn to the brain. Much of the recent interest in mindfulness has come about as a result of the findings of neuroscience. We not only have a pretty good idea of what happens in the brain when we are mindful, but we also have some evidence that practising mindfulness leads to fairly enduring changes in the brain.

This is the most technical and scientific section of the book. You may be tempted to write it off as too complex to grasp, but if you stick with it, we're pretty sure you'll find it as fascinating as we do. But we start, not with complex neuroscience, but with something all of us can know first-hand – what the experience of mindfulness is like, from the inside.

The mindful mind

When I step into an icy rock pool I will sense the cold of the water and the sharpness of the rock on the sole of my foot. If my awareness is intentionally focused on these sensations, I am experiencing a moment of being mindful. I may then have thoughts about that experience; thoughts about whether I've stepped on something dangerous or about how the temperature compares to last week, or whether it is too cold for a swim. Then I am moving out of a mindful state until I notice, with a neutral curiosity, where my mind has wandered to. According to Kirk Brown, Richard Ryan, and David Creswell,[2] a mindful state is one in which awareness is turned towards internal and external stimuli rather than the cognitive processing that takes place in response. Awareness is heightened, and perceptual experiences are stripped bare of prejudice, opinion, evaluation, past experiences, and previously rehearsed emotional responses.

Normally sensory objects are held in consciousness only briefly before we respond with reflection or evaluation. When we are in a mindful state, sensory experience is more strongly attended to and processing largely suspended. The mindful state is achieved more effectively with practice and training, and experienced mindfulness practitioners notice increased intensity of these perceptions and experiences when meditating.

But when we talk about having a mindful mind, we are not only talking about a particular state of consciousness. We can also have a mindful attitude that we can bring to bear on our internal and external experiences as we approach them. Jon Kabat-Zinn[3] has named nine interconnected attitudes that help with this. He lists these as:

- Non-Judging

- Patience

- Beginner's Mind

- Trust

- Non-Striving

- Acceptance

- Letting Go

- Generosity

- Gratitude.

From his perspective, "Non-Striving" encompasses all of them, it is a key aspect of formal mindfulness practice. Non-striving is about staying with our experience as it is rather than trying to change it, escape from it, or fix it. Instead of constantly seeing the gap between where we are and where we would like to be, we stay with what is here in this moment. It is an attitude not just for formal practice but to be cultivated as part of daily life. This is sometimes known as the *informal* practice of mindfulness.

Get Some Exercise!

Eating mindfully

Eating is something we often do on automatic pilot. We might be eating a sandwich at our desk focusing on the computer screen, or barely conscious that we have been snacking all afternoon. This exercise is about noticing what happens when we eat with the intention of being present to our senses.

Choose a piece of fruit.

Hold it in your hand or between your fingers.

Notice the texture and weight as you hold it still or turn it. Focus closely on its visual appearance. Take in the colour, the shape, the different shades and patterns.

When you are ready, take a bite and notice the sensation of doing so on your teeth. What sounds are made? Try to register the sensations on your tongue.

Begin to slowly chew. What flavours do you notice? Can you sense different textures? Do you notice yourself responding any differently to the tougher parts compared with the flesh?

Continue this deliberate focus on this fruit and the sensations it produces as you take the next bite.

Reflect. How was this different to other experiences of eating?

Suppose, for example, we feel anxious about some important exam results that will arrive in the post tomorrow. The experience of anxiety can be unpleasant and we may try to get rid of the emotion either by distracting ourselves or by trying to relax. The action of trying to move away from this experience of anxiety immediately puts us in striving mode as we get caught up in trying to achieve a state of relaxation. In addition to our understandable concern about the results, we are now also caught up in a whirlpool of negative judgments about ourselves.

As you can probably see, *non-striving* is closely linked to *acceptance*. In this sense, acceptance doesn't mean passive resignation or a contrived attempt to like something, it means being open to what is present. Holding our experience of thoughts, images, sensations, and external events in accepting awareness allows us to look closely at what is happening without closing down in instant judgment. "It is a willingness *to see clearly* the facts before us, even if they are difficult to take on board."[4]

Kabat Zinn's *non-judging* attitude is important here. We arrive at situations with all kinds of ideas, memories, or conceptual information that will create a particular story or frame through which we will interpret events. We colour events before they even happen, with like or dislike, danger or safety. Allowing these thoughts to be registered as mental events and paying attention to input from our senses, helps us to gain clarity of awareness. On one memorable occasion, I attended a conference in which mindfulness expert Shaun Lambert asked us to be mindful of the smell and texture of a sample of wild otter faeces. We passed it to each other in a small container, only too aware of our initial disgust. But as we gradually overcame our aversion, we slowly opened our senses to take in the actual smell, which was not inherently unpleasant.

This kind of openness to experience and letting go of preconceptions (or being aware of their presence) is a stepping into *beginner's mind*. That is, arriving somewhere as if for the first time, with a freshness of sight, unclouded by prejudice. This creates possibilities for new discoveries as curiosity enables us to see what we haven't noticed before. In our relationships, we can see new depths or quirks of personality in those who we think we already know, or common ground with people we'd previously boxed as "different". In our working lives, we may notice surprising glimmers of contentment or even joy in jobs normally anticipated with boredom. Taking a leap towards the divine, Joanna Collicutt suggests that in order to receive the illumination of the light of Christ, and to see ourselves and others with his eyes, "we need first to open our minds: to wonder".[5]

But when we open ourselves to experience, it can be difficult to be with what emerges: we may be facing the reality of a cancer diagnosis or the imminent death of a loved one, or the suffering of physical pain. Even benign or pleasant experience can be difficult to attend to. It takes *courage* to let go of obsessive and self-attacking thinking about a past or future event that is niggling us. It takes resolve to focus on the present moment.

What wasn't listed explicitly by Jon Kabat-Zinn, although it is absolutely central to mindfulness practice, is the attitude of *compassion*.[6] Both courage and compassion can be thought of as virtues, and therefore rightfully viewed as aims of Christian discipleship. The virtue of compassion is particularly associated with mindfulness. Once we develop the capacity to "be with" our experiences, it is compassion that allows us to "turn to distress and pain rather than fleeing from it". We will explore this issue in much more depth in later chapters.

The mindful body

One of the reasons we struggle to stay with our present experience, rather than drifting off into thoughts or judgments, is that our minds have a tendency to leap uncontrollably from one thing to another. This has been called "the monkey mind": jumping here and there, and never quite being able to sit still. As a consequence of our hyperactive minds, most mindfulness experts recommend formal routine and regular practice. It has often been asserted that if we want to still the mind, we can start by stilling the body. Attention to breathing and posture are therefore an important part of this.

Mindfulness is practised in order to develop certain habits of mind, with a view to reducing reactive modes of thinking and feeling (for example responding to a twinge of pain with, "Oh no! I'm going to get one of my headaches. I'll miss that meeting and I will let everyone down yet again. Why does this always happen to me? I'm so sick of my life!"), and instead cultivating curiosity (for example, "that's interesting; there's a slight pain in my head... there's also a breeze on my face from the open window... the carpet is blue and has a stain on it...

45

my shoe is pinching somewhat ... "). Increasing general awareness of the body (rather than obsessing about particular physical symptoms) is supported through the use of simple breathing techniques.[7]

By the Book

Present moment awareness

The Bible champions present moment awareness. Although not often made much of in church teaching, it is nevertheless there. When we read the passage in Matthew instructing us not to "worry about tomorrow" (6:25–34), we can view it as a rule about not worrying that can be difficult to obey. But if we see it as permission to embrace the present moment, and to trust that our Father knows our needs, it can more helpfully enable us to be willing to accept the uncertainty of the future.

The mindful attitudes listed here are consistent with much of the teaching of Jesus. The idea of "beginner's mind" or a preparedness to see afresh without prejudice is vital in seeing who Jesus is: "Whether he is a sinner or not, I don't know. One thing I do know. I was blind but now I see!" (John 9:25). The blind man whom Jesus heals in John chapter 9 can now "see". He is not only given literal sight but enabled to recognize that Jesus comes from God, in contrast to the Pharisees who are blind to this truth.

This notion of seeing is repeated throughout the Gospels and refers not only to seeing Jesus but also to seeing others and ourselves; seeing our own weakness enough to see others without prejudice. As in Matthew 7:5 (NRSV) – "You hypocrite, first take the log out of your own eye, and then you will see clearly to take the speck out of your neighbour's eye."

Being still in mind and body is an important key to mindfulness, even if it is not the whole of it. Mindfulness practitioners are usually encouraged to develop a formal practice by finding a place at home or in nature where they can sit regularly and practise without disturbance. Usually this requires a designated space and a regular time. People are encouraged to practise daily for between thirty and forty minutes. These are habits which need to be built up over a period of time. Perhaps the most common body posture is to sit on a straight-backed chair with one's feet flat on the ground, one's back straight and not supported by the chair so that alertness is maintained, palms resting relaxed in one's lap, and eyes closed.

A helpful tool for the stillness of the body and mind is a focus on the breath. All that is required is that we watch ourselves breathing, in and out, without trying to change in any way our breathing patterns. Sometimes it may be useful to narrow attention down even further: we can focus on our breath as it enters and leaves the nostrils, or as it enters and leaves our chest or belly.

Anxiety can cause us to develop shallow breathing. In mindfulness practice, we are often encouraged to develop abdominal breathing, breathing like singers or public speakers, from the belly rather than the chest. Of course, the mind will wander when we try to focus on the breath. The task then is to return awareness gently back to the breath, while maintaining an attitude of curiosity, openness, acceptance, and compassion.[8] Our thoughts will inevitably rush in and distract us from our focus on the breath, many times during one sitting. But when the mind wanders, we continue to bring it back over and over again, with gentleness and self-compassion.

For some people this awareness of the body is a new thing. Many of us live discombobulated lives, out of tune with our bodies. People who are workaholics often say that it is only when they become ill, when they succumb to flu or a cold that they realize how tired they are. When developing a mindful practice, one of the first exercises that newcomers are taught is to bring awareness to the body via the body scan method. The body scan has been shown to be very useful in treating anxiety and pain. In the body scan we are encouraged to turn the spotlight of our attention to various parts of the body. Starting with the left foot and ending at the top of the head, we are encouraged to move our focus slowly upward, noticing itching, tingling, heaviness, lightness, warmth, cold, and more.[9]

Get Some Exercise!

Focus on the breath

Paying attention to our breath can be a helpful anchor to the present. The emphasis in this exercise is to practise returning to the present focus with a kind authority rather than self-criticism when the mind has wandered.

Set a timer for five minutes.

Sit in an upright chair with your feet flat on the floor and your arms placed comfortably. Allow your eyes to close.

Pay attention to your breath, notice the various sensations as you inhale and exhale. You may focus on your nostrils or the movement of your abdomen. Notice where else in your body there are changes as you breathe. There is no need to change your breathing in any way. Your task is just to notice.

When your mind wanders from your breath take note of where your mind has travelled. Were you planning? Replaying a past conversation? Engaging in an imagined dialogue? Note what it was you were thinking about, remembering that minds do wander. Once you have noted where your mind has gone, gently but firmly and with self-compassion bring your mind back to the breath.

When your time is up, allow your eyes to open and bring your attention back to your physical surroundings.

It is often helpful to do the body scan listening to a guided meditation. We bring our attention to the sole of the left foot: feeling its contact with the ground, the toes, the ball of the foot, the arch and Achilles tendon, and the left ankle. Then we focus on the lower left leg: the calf, the shin, and the connection to the left knee. Then moving the awareness to the thigh and the left hip, and then withdrawing attention from the left leg and placing it on the bottom of the right foot and so on until we reach the top of the head.

The task of this exercise is not to analyse, change, or fix; it is merely to be attentive and aware of the body in the here and now. Thus someone who is feeling anxious might become aware of tightness in the chest or pain in the head; being simply aware but not trying to change anything, continuing to sit still. This is the challenge of mindfulness practice.

The body scan is particularly effective in treating chronic and enduring pain.[10] While short-lived pain may require medication and other physical treatments, it is thought that chronic pain has psychological aspects. It is therefore important to work with thoughts and feelings as well as the sensation of pain itself. The body scan, as described above, can be the first step in identifying the part of the body that is holding the pain and tension. The second step is to modify the emotional reaction to the pain, learning to live in the here and now and deal with the pain moment by moment. Bringing mindful attention to emotions of sadness, anger, or despair that accompany the experience of pain, involves learning to sit with uncomfortable emotions rather than resisting or fighting them. We learn to let them be. The task is simply to acknowledge that the pain is there even if it is not easy to accept, and to let it be rather than attempting to let it go.[11]

This brings us to the controversial question of whether Christians should practise yoga. It has to be acknowledged that yoga's aspiration to integrate body and mind is an important reminder of something Western Christianity has often forgotten. At times it has not only neglected the body but viewed it as inherently sinful, and we can be grateful for the reminder to reconnect with the body. We can learn from yoga without having to take on board the entire world view that underpins it.

As a Sanskrit term, Yoga simply means to "concentrate" or to "yoke". In mindful yoga the aim is to "yoke" both body and the mind, and draw them together into one concentrated focus. This makes sense because, although Western thinking in recent centuries has tended to separate the body and mind, they are not independent entities. Christianity has always understood the soul to be embodied, and after death we will not be disembodied spirits but spiritual bodies (1 Corinthians 15).

While it may not be possible to get seriously into yoga without to some extent taking on board its underlying world view, it can still be acknowledged that some aspects of yoga have a lot in common with ancient traditional Christian bodily meditation. The current interest in yoga should act as a stimulus for Christians to rediscover old or develop new body-based Christian spiritual practices, some of which are covered in the next chapter.

The mindful brain

It goes without saying of course that the human brain is part of the human body. We are used to the idea of the brain being the author of our thoughts, feelings, and actions; but it's equally true that what we do, and the way we think and feel, can change our brain. It's a two-way street. There is, it turns out, some truth in the idea of mind (or mindfulness) over matter. But what sort of matter are we talking about?

The brain is an electro-chemical organ. It is made up of two basic sorts of cells: *neurons* and *glia*. Neurons are specialized to pass information to each other in chains or networks. They use up an enormous amount of energy for their size and are powered, supported, and protected by the glia cells. Messages are passed between individual neurons by means of brain chemicals: *neurotransmitters*. These are released into the gaps between the neurons: the *synapses*. The trigger for releasing the neurotransmitter is an electrical current, which in its turn occurred in response to neurotransmitters from other neurons. It is a kind of electro-chemical relay like a series of beacons:

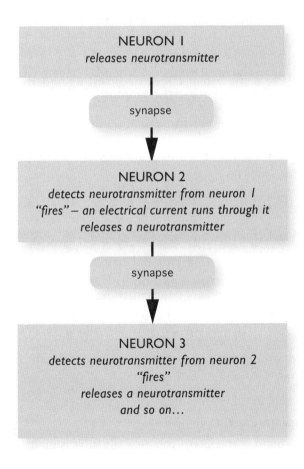

Networks of neurons can change when we are learning new skills and habits, and we would expect something similar for the brains of people who are skilled at meditation. How do these networks change? There are several different mechanisms for these changes, including:

- *Synaptogenesis*: Neurons that *fire* together *wire* together – they develop synaptic connections.

- *Neurogenesis*: Neural stem cells can be stimulated to create new neurons in the brain. This takes 6–12 weeks.

- *Myelinogenesis*: glia cells wind myelin (a fatty substance that acts as an electrical insulator) around connected neurons to increase the speed of the neurons' activity by up to 300 times.

Neuroscientific inquiry into mindfulness is at an early stage, and most research findings have yet to be replicated. Nevertheless some consistent findings are emerging.

Help... I'm a Geek

Further reading in this area

A self-help book introducing the reader to mindfulness. It includes a CD with mindfulness meditations that are similar to (but shorter than) those offered on an eight-week Mindfulness Based Cognitive Therapy (MBCT) course:

Williams, J. M. G. & Penman, D. (2011). *Mindfulness: A Practical Guide to Finding Peace in a Frantic World*. London: Piatkus.

This book describes each session of the eight-week course and how MBCT came to be developed:

Segal, Z. V., Williams, J. M. G. & Teasdale, J. D. (2002). *Mindfulness-Based Cognitive Therapy for Depression: A New Approach to Preventing*

Relapse. New York: Guilford Press.

Guided meditations can be accessed via an app or online via Headspace.com, co-founded by Andy Puddicome and mentioned in the introduction: www.headspace.com

A book whose subject is trauma but which gives some helpful insights in the way emotions work through our brains and bodies:

Van der Kolk, B. (2015). *The Body Keeps the Score: Brain, Mind, and Body in the Healing of Trauma.* London: Penguin.

A complete list of sources is provided in the reference section at the end of the book.

The studies use *functional imaging* techniques such as fMRI (functional magnetic resonance imaging) and PET (positron emission tomography).[12] These are ways of recording the activity of different parts of the brain by measuring the amount of energy they are using up. The studies look at two main questions. First, are there characteristic brain changes when people practise being intentionally non-reactive by simply labelling their experiences in the non-judgmental way described by Kabat-Zinn? Second, do people who practise mindful meditation develop longer-term brain changes?[13]

Studies looking at the first question have found that mindful non-reactive labelling of experience is accompanied by increased activity in the *prefrontal cortex* (an area involved with self-control) and decreased activity in parts of the brain involved with experiencing and expressing emotion (such as the *amygdala*).[14] This pattern of brain activity is what we would expect to find when a person is engaged in some sort of intentional self-regulation and where emotional reactivity has been reduced.

There is evidence that these brain changes in turn suppress the *body's* emotional response (for example by inhibiting the production of stress hormones such as cortisol by the adrenal glands in the kidneys). This reduces the intensity of the physical aspects of emotional experience.[15] Experienced mindful meditators also show some distinctive changes in brain activity[16] including increased release of the neurotransmitter dopamine, which is usually associated with experience of pleasure.

Studies looking at the question of longer-term brain changes in mindfulness practitioners have found that mindfulness training appears to increase connectivity between the prefrontal cortex and insular cortex (which lies underneath the frontal area and is thought to register *gut* feelings).[17] The increased connectivity between these two centres may contribute to a strengthening of a set of "executive circuits" whose functions range from bodily regulation to social understanding. They are "profoundly *integrative*, linking widely spread areas to each other".[18] The individual parts of these circuits are not special but their power lies in their ability to bring the nervous system into a functional whole ("neural integration"). In doing so, they enable highly complex aspects of human functioning from emotional balance to empathy and moral behaviour.[19]

In summary, there is growing evidence for some specific changes in the prefrontal cortex, insular cortex, and amygdala as a result of mindfulness training, together with the development of a particular pattern of connections between them. These anatomical structures are known to mediate psychological functions that underlie the objectives of mindfulness so this makes sense.

Mindfulness is a state of mind–body–brain

In this chapter we've looked at mindfulness as an aspect of human functioning – a biologically based way of being in the world, either as a short-term practice, a longer-term skill, or an enduring attitude. We've seen that it is basically a form of self-regulation that can offer the opportunity to increase well-being by enabling its practitioners to direct their attention to the right things in the right way. In particular it allows them to inhabit the present moment fully without being dominated by regrets for the past or worries about the future. As a human capacity we would expect it to turn up in different guises in different cultures and faith traditions. We would expect to find something of it in Christianity. In the next chapter we explore whether this is actually the case.

When Two or Three are Gathered...

Questions for group discussion

As a group, try a short meditation together.

Choose an exercise from one of the boxes above, or a meditation from Mindfulness: A Practical Guide to Finding Peace in a Frantic World. Discuss together what you noticed.

Where in the Bible do we receive the message that the present moment is to be embraced?

How has your relationship to Jesus been improved by times of present moment awareness?

What gets in the way of us having a present moment focus?

Where could you do with more awareness of the present moment? And how could you go about practising it?

If mindfulness and meditation are based in the brain does that rule them out of life in the Spirit?

The Mindful Christian

In the previous chapter we saw that mindfulness can be understood as a way of thinking and doing that involves being fully in the present moment without wishing it were otherwise. We have seen that it is something that people do naturally and can also cultivate intentionally. But is it for Christians? Should Christians practise mindfulness?

Now we turn to look at this question, and we will find not only that it is OK for Christians to be mindful, but that this is demanded of us by Jesus himself. This demand was taken up by his followers, beginning in the early centuries after Christ, and then developed over the next few hundred years in the spiritual traditions of the mainstream Western (Roman Catholic) and Eastern (Orthodox) churches. Following the European Reformation in the sixteenth century, these spiritual traditions received little attention from some (though not all) of the emerging Protestant churches, but in the twentieth century they were rediscovered afresh in the evangelical tradition through the writings of people such as Dallas Willard (see www.renovare.org).

Following Jesus

As we read the Gospels we see that Jesus models and teaches an *attitude* to God, the world, and the self before he gets on to dealing with the specifics of how to pray. He lives and prays out of this attitude and, perhaps surprisingly, it turns out to have a lot in common with the way that mindfulness has been described by secular practitioners like Jon Kabat-Zinn. Just to remind you, we can sum up its key aspects as:

1. Trust

2. Gratitude

3. Beginner's mind

4. Not worrying

5. Attentiveness and awareness

6. Non-judging.

Jesus doesn't tell people to practise mindfulness (nor does he forbid it), but he clearly models a mindful attitude. He promotes it not for its own sake or even for our well-being; instead it comes out of his theology – his core beliefs about God:

• God is good

• God is a God of grace

• God reveals himself to humble, open-hearted folk

• God is GOD

• God's kingdom has drawn near

• God has a particular time frame.

With this in mind, let's take a look at the six attitudes listed above, starting with trust.

Trust: the facts are friendly

Jesus insists that God's disposition to humanity is one of goodwill, and when God became human in Jesus we were able to access this goodwill in a new way (Luke 2:14). That's the "good news" of the gospel. It is summed up in Jesus' teaching on prayer, in which he instructs his followers to imitate him in calling God *Abba* (an intimate though not infantile word for "father") and to be bold enough to ask God directly for bread and forgiveness (Matthew 6:9; Mark 14:36; Luke 11:2). God is pleased with his son Jesus (Matthew 3:17; Luke 3:22; Mark 1:11) and, insofar as he is pleased with Jesus, the "last Adam" (after Romans 5:15), he is pleased with all human beings who trust in him. In Jesus, God and human beings are reconciled to each other (Romans 5:1; 2 Corinthians 5:19) yet without God having to drop his standards or act against his holy nature (Romans 3:26).

Where Did it Come From?

Historical roots of practice

We can reconstruct some of the earliest Christian practice from Acts and the New Testament letters, but also from a very early Christian document called the "Didache", which has, for example, its own version of the Lord's Prayer.

The desert fathers and mothers were the Christians who went out into the deserts of Egypt alone to pursue a life of self-denial and contemplation. Their lives and sayings were written down and collected from the fourth century. Many of the sayings of one of these, Evagrius Ponticus (345–399), resonate strongly with a mindful approach; for example, "You cannot attain pure prayer while entangled in material things and agitated by constant cares. For prayer means the shedding of thoughts."

The accounts of Greek monastic practices such as Hesychasm (described later) are preserved in a work called "The Philokalia" (literally "Love of beautiful things"), a four-volume anthology of the spiritual writings of the Eastern church between the fourth and fifteenth centuries.

It's fairly easy to get hold of English translations of these ancient works, and some are listed in the reference section at the end of the book.

Jesus therefore demands that we treat God as utterly trustworthy, in the way an innocent child comes to her parent in a completely open-handed manner (Matthew 7:7–11).

Gratitude: it's a gift

Everything good that we have is a gift from God. This ought to make us happy, but in fact we often just don't get it. We have a deep-seated belief that there are no free lunches – that we have to do something to earn God's gift, or else we treat the gift as a burden. Consider the prodigal son and his brother: one thought he could earn forgiveness through saying words of repentance but was forgiven before he could speak them; the other was working hard at home, not out of affectionate devotion but "like a slave" (Luke 15:29 NRSV) in order to safeguard his inheritance. Neither of them understood that their father's love was a free gift (Romans 5:16).

It's only when we stop kidding ourselves that we are in control and that we can make things happen through our skill or power, that we start to understand that we are to accept all God's gifts with thanks, not grasp at them as things we have earned. This is really the nature of human faith; it is a turning to God with the insight that we have nothing other than what has been given to us. Jesus commended the woman who washed his feet for her faith (Luke 7:50), and he explained this in terms of her loving gratitude for the gift of God that, as a notorious "sinner", she could not possibly have earned herself.

Gratitude is about saying "thank you", and Jesus often did this. But more fundamentally it's a right way of seeing the world, of tuning in to it, of *receiving* (John 1:12, 16).

Beginner's mind: becoming like little children

Small children begin life with an attitude of trust, which they may sadly have to unlearn in the light of bad experiences at the hands of adults. They also understand that they have nothing and need all. They are open-hearted and approach adults with open hands. Jesus repeatedly commends a childlike attitude. In order to enter the kingdom of God adults need to become like children, to go back and be born afresh (Matthew 18:3; John 3:3–5). He also gives thanks to God that the gospel is received best by children (Matthew 11:25).

By the Book

Keeping watch

We've seen that in a Christian context, a mindful attitude is one that is alert and ready for action but also needs the patience to be responsive to God's timing. Thomas Keating talks about a "Here I am" attitude – a way of placing oneself at God's disposal. This seems to be what Jesus was asking of his disciples in Gethsemane when he told them to "keep watch" (Mark 14:27, 34).

Perhaps the best example of this watchfulness comes from someone with a "beginner's mind" and an open attitude of trust – the child Samuel, who in the watches of the night heard the voice of God and famously responded "hinneh!" – "Here I am!" (1 Samuel 3:4). The word "hinneh" would therefore be a highly appropriate choice as a sacred word for "centering prayer" (described later).

Intentionally taking on a beginner's mind (what the philosopher Paul Ricoeur would call a "second naiveté") means that we approach life with little or nothing in the way of emotional, intellectual, or material baggage. We come with no preconceptions to limit us. We come humbly, free to ask "stupid" questions. Above all, we come in wonder.

Not worrying: God is GOD

A key aspect of beginner's mind is travelling light. Again and again Jesus talks about the way possessions and wealth stop people from living out the gospel (Matthew 19:24; 6:19–21) because we tend to want to hold onto them (Luke 12:16–21). He warns against over-investment in family relationships (Luke 14:26). He criticizes the leaders of his day for their preoccupation with religion, and he even has a go at one of his own disciples, Martha (Luke 10:41), for being preoccupied with serving him! All of these things – even wealth – are good in their place. Jesus' point is that they can so easily claim our attention and turn into idols. They can become a source of *worry*.

Once we start worrying, filling our minds with all the things that could go wrong, it is hard for us to hear the voice of God or to notice the needs of others (Matthew 6:33–34). Our very worry is an indication that we are relying on our own resources rather than trusting that God is on our side and in charge (Matthew 6:31–32). Of course, there are times when planning and problem-solving are an important part of responsible living; but we need to know when and how to set this aside.

Attentiveness and awareness: consider the lilies

Much of Jesus' teaching is based on his close observation of nature – a noticing of the germination and growth of tiny seeds, of yeast mixed into flour, of salt sprinkled on food, of sparrows that fall, of children who wonder. It's really interesting to see how he uses this approach to challenge the human tendency to worry. He tells his disciples to stop and pay attention to the birds and wild flowers (Matthew 6:25–29), things that as followers of the messiah they might have thought beneath their consideration. Later in the Temple, he tells them to notice an unobtrusive widow (Mark 12:42–44) while they are distracted by the magnitude and glory of its architecture (Mark 13:1). Above all, he contrasts Martha's worry over serving him with Mary's stillness and attentiveness to him, saying that, on this occasion at least, she "has chosen what is better" (Luke 10:42).

Jesus' story of the Good Samaritan is instructive here because it seems to set up a link between attentiveness and compassion. We aren't told why the priest and Levite ignore a man lying injured on the road, but we might infer that it is because they are preoccupied. This is plausible because the story comes immediately before the account of Martha's preoccupation and Mary's attentiveness in chapter 10 of Luke's Gospel, so the two may well be linked.

In 1973 two psychologists, John Darley and Dan Batson, carried out an experiment based on the Good Samaritan story.[1] It involved sixty-seven students at Princeton Theological Seminary. The students were asked to prepare a talk that would be given in another building. One group of students prepared a talk on the Good Samaritan and the other group prepared a talk on the career prospects for graduates of the college. They then set off to deliver their talk and were given a map to help them find their way. Half the students in each group were told that they would need to hurry because they were running late. The route went past an alley where a man was slumped down, eyes closed and not moving. As each student went past him, he coughed and groaned once.

Help... I'm a Geek

Further reading in this area

For an accessible account of the rediscovery of ancient Christian disciplines in modern times see:

Foster, R. (2008). *Celebration of Discipline: The Path to Spiritual Growth.* London: Hodder (many versions available).

For an introduction to some of the ideas behind different forms of Christian meditation:

McCullough, D. (2014). *Silence: A Christian History.* London: Penguin.

An ambitious and attractive attempt to reinvent the Liturgy of the Hours for use today can be found in a three-volume work:

Tickle, P. (2001–6). *The Divine Hours.* New York: Doubleday.

A good account of the Jesus Prayer:

Barrington-Ward, S. (2007). *The Jesus Prayer.* Oxford: BRF.

On the desert fathers and mothers see:

Williams, R. (2004). *Silence and Honeycakes: The Wisdom of the Desert.* Oxford: Lion.

For a general introduction to Eastern Orthodox Christianity:

Louth, A. (2013). *Introducing Eastern Orthodox Theology.* London: SPCK.

A complete list of sources is provided in the reference section at the end of the book.

Darley and Batson were shocked to find that overall only 40 per cent of these Christian students stopped to offer to help the man. Surprisingly, preparing a talk on the Good Samaritan didn't make stopping more likely. The only predictor was whether or not the student had been told to hurry. Those who were in a hurry were significantly less likely to stop – they were worried about being late. It seems that worry – even worry in a good cause – not only works against prayerful attentiveness to God but also against compassion towards other people.

Non-judging: now is not the time

Straight after telling people not to worry in the Sermon on the Mount, Jesus goes on to issue the instruction "Do not judge" (Matthew 7:1). Paul takes this theme up at some length in Romans chapter 2. The issue is in part hypocrisy: who are we to set ourselves up as judges when we ourselves are at fault? But more fundamentally it's about understanding God's time frame, something already mentioned in our first chapter. The Greek of the New Testament has two words for time: *chronos* and *kairos*. *Chronos* refers to something like clock time, but *kairos* refers to timely time – the apt moment, the window of opportunity, the ripe time. That's why harvest is such a common image in the Bible; you have to wait for it, it can't be rushed, it doesn't automatically abide by the clock and calendar, and it has to be finely judged.

We need to learn to be patient, trusting *God* to judge at the point when he is good and ready. Jesus understood himself to be inaugurating a judgment-free zone: "the year of the Lord's favour" (Luke 4:19), where people have a chance to turn to God; what's more he understood his mission as offering them a means of doing so (Luke 19:10). The first Christians believed that Jesus would come back very soon as judge, and much of the New Testament is about how to wait patiently for this, to keep alert, to watch and pray.

We still believe that Jesus will return, but with the hindsight of 2,000 years we have ceased to live as if it's going to happen tomorrow. For the present, we try to live out God's justice on earth, and we are under the authority of human judicial systems. Where these are good and informed by Christian principles, as in the UK, they keep in check our personal desires for reactive and rough justice. They help us to wait for ultimate justice. The need to be patient in this, and in many areas of our life where we wait on God's timing, is as vital as ever. Indeed patience is a fruit of the Spirit (Galatians 5:22).

Pray without ceasing:
the early years after Jesus

We don't know very much about the prayer life of the first Christians, though there is evidence that each church tended to do its own thing. This isn't surprising given the limitations of communication channels between the different communities of faith scattered across the Roman empire and beyond. However, some customs seem to have been pretty universal: praying a version of the Lord's Prayer; singing spiritual songs and hymns; reciting the psalms and meditating upon them; the use of the phrase *Marana Tha* (meaning "Our Lord, Come!" or perhaps "Our Lord has come!"); and prayers of thanksgiving at the breaking of bread.

Paul's instruction from 1 Thessalonians 5:17 to pray "constantly" or "without ceasing" was taken very seriously, if not literally. This, together with the well-established Jewish practice of praying and meditating at set times throughout the day and night (Psalm 63:6; Daniel 6:10; Acts 10:3, 9), formed the basis for the development of the "Liturgy of the Hours" – the practice of praying at seven set points in one 24-hour period. The idea behind this was twofold: first to acknowledge that time is a gift from God and is under his authority, and second to embrace the circadian rhythms of human sleep and wakefulness and the setting and rising of the sun as pointing to the pattern of death and resurrection that had been revealed in Christ. This sort of prayer was therefore highly embodied, literally biological (following the logic of life), connected with and mindfully attentive to the natural world, and so very much in line with the teaching of Jesus outlined earlier in this chapter. Thankfully it has been discovered afresh in our generation with the 24-7 prayer movement (www.24-7prayer.com).

The Lord's Prayer has always been central to Christian prayer. As we have seen, it encapsulates an attitude of childlike trust, and encourages the setting aside of worries as the individual and community turn to their heavenly Father. Moreover, in Paul's churches at least, the practice of praying to God as *Abba* was seen as a mark of the indwelling of the Holy Spirit (Romans 8:15; Galatians 4:6).

But as well as praying to God the Father, it seems that the earliest Christians also naturally found themselves praying to Jesus. Of course we do this quite naturally today, but at the time this would have felt like a radical move, especially for Jews. This is almost certainly one way that the first followers of Jesus worked out that Jesus was God – they found that they were worshipping him. It's here that we find the origins of what became distinctively Christian rather than Jewish meditation.

Be still and know that I am God

In Judaism there was a long-established practice of meditating upon the Law: "Blessed is the one who does not walk in step with the wicked or stand in the way that sinners take or sit in the company of mockers, but whose delight is in the law of the Lord, and who meditates on his law day and night" (Psalm 1:1–2). This sometimes involved the use of a prayer shawl (Numbers 15:37–41),[2] and by the time of Jesus there was a practice in some circles of meditating in order to enter into altered states of consciousness; it was believed that this enabled the practitioner to rise above earthly concerns and glimpse a vision of heavenly reality. It is likely that Paul practised this sort of meditation, and he seems to be referring to it in 2 Corinthians 12:2.

The first Christians understood Jesus to have both fulfilled and replaced the Law (Romans 3:21; 10:4; 2 Corinthians 3; 4:6), or to be the Law incarnate (John 1:17), and so they began to explore what it would mean to meditate on *him*. The earliest recorded[3] approach is known as the Jesus Prayer. It goes like this:

Lord Jesus Christ, Son of God, have mercy on me [a sinner].

This is a deceptively simple prayer, deeply grounded in the Bible. It is based on the words of the tax collector in Luke's Gospel (Luke 18:13), and in its attitude to prayer it is obedient to the teaching of Jesus in that passage. But there is a crucial difference: Jesus was teaching about prayer to God, but this prayer is addressed to Jesus himself. This may have first arisen almost unconsciously through incorporating into the prayer the early Christian habit of saying "Lord have mercy!" (*kurie eleēson* in Greek); in the early church this phrase was taken to be a sign of faith on the part of the believer (e.g. Matthew 15:22, 28). Later, as the Jesus Prayer became the basis of meditation, the words took on another more deliberate function.

In the ancient world, as in many places today, people were frightened of entering altered states of consciousness because they believed that this opened the door to the world of the spirits – including demons. For example, people were afraid when they sneezed and particularly afraid of falling asleep without calling on the protection of God. As Christians developed their own practices of meditation, which seemed to open them up to a new area of experience, they too wanted to protect themselves from evil spirits; the obvious way to do this was to call on the *Holy Spirit*. In 1 Corinthians 12:3 Paul had said that no one could call Jesus Lord other than by the Holy Spirit, so what better way to invoke the Spirit than by beginning a period of meditation with the words "Lord Jesus Christ"?

Yes... but...

Should Christians be wasting their time on meditation when they could be praying?

Christian meditation is *one* way of beginning contemplative prayer. It is designed to remove obstacles that get in the way of our being attentive to God, of our looking at and listening to him in adoration (rather than talking to him or presenting him with a list of requests). So, it is not an alternative to prayer but a way into prayer. But it's not the only way in, and it may not be for everyone.

On the other hand, as we have seen, a mindful *attitude* is more than engaging in specific mindful practices; it's about the way we live the whole of our lives, and this attitude is demanded of all Christians.

It was in this context that the practice of "hesychasm" developed. This is most fully documented in the writings of early Greek monks, but something like it was practised by the solitary

Christians who went out into the deserts of Egypt to pursue a life of self-denial and contemplation. Hesychasm (which means stillness) is a type of meditation that was often carried out in the foetal posture as a mark of humility – childlike and with downcast eyes like the tax collector. The Jesus Prayer was used as a mantra to anchor attention, and slow, deep breathing was used to reduce arousal. Any extraneous thoughts and bodily sensations that entered awareness were simply considered in a detached manner and then set aside. We can see connections with both yoga and mindfulness in this ancient Christian practice. Through it practitioners hoped to develop what they called "nepsis", a kind of watchful and mindful attentiveness to the work of God in their lives and in the world.

From meditation to contemplation

Hesychasm was not mistaken for prayer, but was meant to be a kind of mental and spiritual ground-clearing that enabled its practitioners to set aside worry, worldly concerns, and the ego, so that they would then be ready to pray. Some have likened it to loosening the soil so that it may better receive the seed of God's Spirit (Mark 4:8). Unlike meditation, which is basically about cultivating a state of mind, *Christian prayer is always relational.* Christian meditation is done under the authority of God and in obedience to him, but as it moves forward into contemplative prayer the I–Thou relationship with the triune God of love becomes paramount. This is something that was particularly stressed by the sixteenth-century Spanish nun Teresa of Avila in her writings, especially *The Way of Perfection*.[4] Her point was that the only way to God is via a relationship with Jesus Christ that is based on grace, but there are many ways to Jesus and many ways of deepening our relationship with him. Meditation can be a great help but, like reading the Bible or any other spiritual practice, it is a way of transitioning into relational contemplative prayer and should not be a substitute for it.

Receiving the gift of the present moment

Evidence of mindful Christian spiritual practices, whether they involve the focused meditation of Hesychasm or a more general attitude to the life of faith, can be found throughout Christian history. One of the most interesting is the medieval German friar known as Meister Eckhart. His writings deeply influenced Martin Luther and hence the Protestant Reformation. Eckhart insisted that Christians should develop the capacity to sit lightly in relation to all things, including their thoughts, and especially their thoughts about God. Instead, trusting in God's invisible presence, we are to come to a mentally still point, what he called a "*Gelassenheit*" or complete letting-be:

> *We ought not to have or let ourselves be satisfied with the God we have thought of, for when the thought slips the mind, that God slips with it. [This discipline] requires effort and love, a careful cultivation of the spiritual life, and a watchful, honest, active oversight of all one's mental attitudes toward things and people. It is not to be learned by world-flight, running away from things, turning solitary and going apart from the world. Rather, one must learn an inner solitude, wherever or with whomsoever he may be.*[5]

Part of this letting-be is about being fully in the present without wishing it were different (sound familiar?). This is sometimes referred to as "the sacrament of the present moment". This phrase is associated with the French Jesuit Jean-Pierre de Caussade

(1675–1751), who wrote a book with that title. De Caussade argued that Christians do God's will not by anxiously searching for it, not by deliberately resigning ourselves to it, but simply by receiving what comes to us moment by moment and choosing to accept it as God's will for us at this present time, which is in reality all we actually have. He saw the present moment as the point at which God reveals himself to the individual who is called at that instant to act in accordance with it.

This sacrament of the present or *kairos* moment is described as "the pearl of great price" by the Christian poet, R. S. Thomas (1913–2000) in his poem "The Bright Field", where he writes that we should come to see the present moment as a gateway to eternity. In other words – God is *now*.

"New treasures as well as old":[7] Christian meditation in the twenty-first century

The mindful approach to meditation and prayer is so strong in the whole 2,000 years of the Christian tradition that there is not enough room here to give a full history. Much of it comes under the umbrella of what is called the "apophatic" tradition. This is based on the idea that discursive thinking, ideas, and images get in the way of God and are potentially idolatrous and oppressive. This tradition stands in tension with the "kataphatic" tradition that holds that it is precisely through words that God reveals himself – ultimately through Jesus the Word made flesh, but also through the ideas, propositions, and dogmas set out in Scripture. In a mature spirituality the apophatic and kataphatic approaches should come together and balance each other. This does seem to be the case for the spiritual giants of Christian history; for example Meister Eckhart was a superb academic biblical scholar.

The problem is that for the last three centuries with the rise of modernity and literacy, and then the industrial and technological revolutions, there has for the most part been an overemphasis on words and ideas in Western culture. Western Christians, perhaps especially Protestant evangelical Christians, have let the threads of the apophatic tradition slip through their fingers. It has taken the rise in popularity of secular mindfulness to remind us of something we should never have forgotten.

Instead of simply going back to the old ways, some contemporary Christian spiritual writers have brought together aspects of ancient practices and made them accessible to modern-day Christians of all traditions. Perhaps the most promising and famous of these methods is "Centering prayer" which is most strongly associated with Thomas Keating, an American Trappist monk.[8] Several writers have observed strong similarities between centering prayer and aspects of mindfulness-based cognitive therapy.[9] Centering prayer takes some of the principles of mindfulness (for example the gentle letting go of elaborative cognitive processing) but goes further and uses a "sacred word"[10] to centre the practitioner and gently draw her wandering attention back to the triune God. There is an expectation that as she opens her heart and mind to God she will become more aware of his presence and better able to cooperate with his activity in her life. What begins as meditation is therefore meant to move gradually into active contemplative prayer which has real-life consequences for the believer and her community.

When Two or Three are Gathered...

Questions for group discussion

You may like to use the following questions to discuss the issues raised in this chapter as a small group.

How important are the different types of prayer (contemplation, petition, confession, colloquial prayer (chatting to God), praise in English or tongues) to different members of the group? Do group members think that Christian meditation could help or hinder their prayer life?

How does contemplation relate to action in the experience of the group?

What does it mean to become "like little children" (Matthew 18:3) and why does Jesus give this such importance?

Read through the lyrics of "Here I am to worship" by Tim Hughes and reflect together on what a "Here I am" attitude is actually like.

Being Christian

Compassion

Turning to the Compassionate God

The Lord your God is with you,
the Mighty Warrior who saves.
He will take great delight in you;
in his love he will no longer rebuke you,
but will rejoice over you with singing.
(Zephaniah 3:17)

Does God like me?

One evening the minister of a thriving city-centre church asked his large congregation to "Raise your hand if you think God loves you." The majority put their hands straight up. He then asked them to "Raise your hand if you think God likes you?" A much smaller number of people raised their hands. Why would this be? It is possible that our heads know that saying "Yes" to "God loves us" is the right answer. We hear it in Sunday school, we hear it from the front of church, and we read it in the Bible. On the other hand, the word "like" as a description of God's affection for us is not so familiar. When asked this question, we have to search a different part of ourselves for the answer.

By the Book

"I am..."

For the Christian, of course, the Bible is the primary source of images of God. We can learn a lot from the systematic approach taken by Jesus in John's Gospel with his seven "I am" sayings. Look at the verses below and consider what each image tells you about the character and nature of God:

"I am the bread of life." (John 6:35)

"I am the light of the world." (John 8:12)

"I am the gate for the sheep." (John 10:7)

"I am the Good shepherd." (John 10:11)

"I am the resurrection and the life." (John 11:25)

"I am the way and the truth and the life." (John 14:6)

"I am the true vine, and my Father is the gardener." (John 15:1)

As you reflect on them, what kind of relationship do you imagine having with the aspect of God represented by each image?

Results from psychological research show that our *head* knowledge of God can sometimes be quite different to our *heart* knowledge – *felt experience* – of God. Throughout the Bible, God has been described as powerful and strong (Isaiah 40:11), faithful (Exodus 34:6), a refuge and helper (Psalm 46:1), just and righteous (Jeremiah 9:23–24), wise (Job 12:13) and, above all, loving (Deuteronomy 7:9; 1 John 4:8). Yet the experiences of ministers and psychological therapists suggest that for some people a *head* knowledge of God consistent with these Bible verses does not automatically translate into *heart* knowledge. In this chapter we will briefly summarize one of the ways in which this discrepancy may be understood and share some ideas which can be used to enlarge our heart knowledge of God. We outline how mindful practices can act as a foundation for opening up this heart knowledge and as a means to sustain it.

Head and heart knowledge

As creatures, the way we understand and relate to God is mediated by our history and the limitations of our finite minds and bodies. Recognizing this, some psychologists have looked into the way beliefs about God's attributes are actually represented in the mind. In one experiment[1] young adult Christians were given a list of thirty-two adjectives and asked to rate each of them in two ways. Firstly, how much did each word reflect what they "should believe that God is like" (head knowledge about dogma), and secondly, how much did it reflect what they "personally feel God is like" (heart knowledge based on experience)? The participants described God much more positively in "head" mode than they did in "heart" mode. There was a gap between what they knew about the character of God and how they personally experienced him.

When people are able to talk frankly to a therapist or trusted friend it is quite common for them to express frustration or even guilt that they can't experience God's love in the way they feel they should do or would like. As biological, psychological, social, and spiritual beings, there are multiple reasons for this struggle, unique to each individual. Sometimes it is related to a distressing event or life circumstance that has not been fully processed; at other times the person describes a way of relating to God which reflects a wider pattern characteristic of his or her other close relationships.

Attachment to God, the encourager and comforter

One of the most popular theories for understanding our close relationships is "Attachment Theory". Attachment Theory began with the psychiatrist John Bowlby and his observations of children during separations from their primary caregivers (or "attachment figures"). He suggested that humans have an inborn strategy of staying close to an attachment figure in order to reduce distress and provide psychological and physical safety. If this caregiver is able to respond sensitively to her needs, the child will experience her (or him) as a "safe haven" and a "secure base". As a safe haven, the caregiver offers effective soothing when the child is distressed or threatened. As a secure base, the caregiver offers support for curiosity and learning when the child explores the world. No parent is perfect but when these conditions are in place *enough of the time* children develop a trust that the caregiver is available and capable of looking after them. The child will also develop a sense of competence and value. A relationship like this is known as a **secure attachment**.

Attachment researchers have also studied attachments that *don't* provide security. The psychologist Mary Ainsworth meticulously observed separations and reunions of children and their caregivers. She was able to identify two forms of "insecure attachment" in which there is a mismatch between the child's need and the care that is offered. These are often referred to as "avoidant" and "anxious".

In an **anxious attachment**, the mismatch occurs in relation to a child's need for a secure base. A child may have just begun to settle into exploring her surroundings only to have her mother call her back to meet an arbitrary need (such as fixing her hair). The need is to explore, but the mother is drawing her child back to herself. This is unlikely to be intentional or even conscious, but carers in anxious attachments tend to pull their children back from exploration in response to their own emotional needs. For example, a caregiver who feels rejected, guilty, or fearful may prefer to keep the child close because it reduces these painful feelings. When this becomes a repeated pattern, the child receives the message that he "shouldn't have the feelings associated with curiosity, mastery or autonomy"[2] and learns to seek proximity instead of exploration in order to meet the needs of the parent. These templates for relating to others can be carried into adulthood, and those with this kind of early experience tend to fear separation in their adult relationships. Worries about rejection or a preoccupation with what others think can interfere with joyful and confident engagement in work and leisure.

In an **avoidant attachment**, the mismatch happens in relation to a child's need for the caregiver to be a safe haven. Here the parent tends to divert the child towards a toy or task rather than staying with the child, maintaining their closeness, or responding directly to distress. When caregivers are uncomfortable providing comfort and soothing when the child is in distress, the child learns that she "shouldn't have the feelings associated with needing safety and closeness"[3] and will turn to exploration rather than proximity. If this pattern is maintained, the adult is likely to struggle with closeness to others and lean towards "compulsive self-reliance".[4]

Because these early relationship patterns influence how we function in adult relationships it is not surprising that some psychologists have considered how this might apply to our relationship with God. These psychologists are very clear that they are not trying to "explain God away". They are simply exploring how people bring their early experiences of relationship to their relationship with God. Even the Bible tends to speak of God as an attachment figure – as both secure base and safe haven. We talk about our "relationship with God", about seeking God in times of need, and gaining confidence for tackling difficulties through a sense of his presence.

What we are talking about here is our *heart* knowledge of God and how this may be affected by our early parental attachment patterns. Research suggests that this "felt" experience of God will *correspond* to our early experience with our caregivers. People with insecure early attachments may find it hard to trust God, and experience him as distant, absent, or demanding and capricious – *even when their head knowledge* tells them that God is supposed to be trustworthy, consistent, accessible, and compassionate. This "correspondence", however, is not inevitable. Certainly we know many who have endured significant early deprivation or trauma who report a strong felt experience of God's love. Conversely, those who have enjoyed secure attachments early in life may nevertheless struggle to know God as intimately as they would like. The distance between a person's head and heart knowledge will be influenced by multiple events, not least the passage of time as a faith journey unfolds.

We have summarized attachment theory because it can be a useful tool in thinking about how we relate to God. It helps us reflect on our "attachment behaviours" and our mental image of God, sometimes known as our *God-representation*. Is it possible to know and trust God as a safe haven, a *comforter*, even when we have not experienced this from our own caregivers? Can we come to God in times of threat, distress, sin, or weakness, without hiding (like Adam and Eve), walking in the opposite direction, or trying to make it better first? Are we able to trust that we will be met with compassion, tenderness, and acceptance, even when facing painful realities? Or do we heap on excessive remorse in the belief that only this will make us acceptable?

What about God as a secure base or as *encourager*? Can we sense God supporting our curiosity and autonomy? The idea that God wants to support our autonomy is expressed by C. S. Lewis when Screwtape advises, "He wants them to learn to walk and must therefore take away His hand; and if only the will to walk is really there He is pleased even with their stumbles."[5] Can we trust God's strength and wisdom as he delights in our explorations as one who "led them with cords of human kindness, with ties of love" (Hosea 11:4)?

As creatures, there will inevitably be limitations in our capacity to embrace the full truth of who God is, but understanding something of our own psychology may help us move closer to it. As we notice the gap between our head and heart knowledge, is it possible to know that God is with us in this? He knows even better than we do what life circumstances have contributed to it. Can we give ourselves permission to consider how our heart knowledge might grow? Psychology tells us that beliefs change most effectively when we *experience* a new perspective rather than simply receive it in words. Some experiential tools are therefore shared below that may be beneficial in cultivating a more compassionate, and therefore more accurate, heart knowledge of God.

Being-with: attachment and mindfulness

Quite a few researchers have noted that our capacity for mindfulness and our attachment security are linked. Having a foundation of secure attachment may make it easier to be mindful, because securely attached people carry within themselves a loving attachment figure which allows them to "remain mindful of what is happening within and around them"[6] even when things are stressful.

Help... I'm a Geek

Further reading in this area

To understand more about attachment theory and an excellent parenting intervention:

Powell, B., Cooper, G., Hoffman, K. & Marvin, B. (2013). *The Circle of Security Intervention. Enhancing Attachment in Early Parent–Child Relationships*. New York: The Guilford Press.

See also: www.circleofsecurity.net

For a more academic study of the way early experience affects our God-representations:

Kirkpatrick, L. (2004). *Attachment, Evolution, and the Psychology of Religion*. New York: Guilford.

Rizzuto, A.-M. (1979). *The Birth of the Living God: A Psychoanalytic Study*. Chicago, IL: Chicago University Press.

For an exploration of using art to help explore the visual aspects of our God-representations:

Persson, A. (2010). *The Circle of Love: Praying with Rublev's Icon of the Trinity*. Oxford: BRF.

A complete list of sources is provided in the reference section at the end of the book.

It is striking that both mindfulness and attachment literature emphasize the importance of "being with" whatever happens to arise. *Being-with* is the term used by Bert Powell and colleagues to describe the emotional availability of the caregiver to the child, whatever the need, whether comforting closeness or support in exploration. *Being-with* is more than just providing proximity. It is about communicating to the child that he is known, that his needs are acceptable, and offering empathy to help him regulate overwhelming feelings. This helps the child to know that "hurts can be hurts, wants can be wants, angers and joys and requests can be just what they are – nothing more and nothing less".[7]

We mentioned earlier the idea that those with anxious attachments learn to avoid feelings associated with *curiosity, mastery*, or *autonomy*, and those with avoidant attachments learn to avoid feelings associated with *needing safety and closeness*. Neither have developed the capacity for emotional regulation that comes with repeated experiences of others tuning into and resonating with the full range of our emotions: *being-with* us as we feel rather than trying to fix. This tuning in gives the message that feelings are not dangerous and will eventually pass. In a similar way the practice of mindfulness teaches us to tune in to ourselves with compassion. As mindfulness practitioners, Christina Feldman and Willem Kuyken suggest, "… compassion begins with the discovery of the capacity to 'be with', to be steady and balanced in the face of adversity".[8]

Of course, as Christians, we can choose to look to ourselves for emotional regulation, but we can also be intentional about asking God to be with us in any emotional state that bothers us, whether pleasant or unpleasant. God is the essence of *being-with*. Unlike a human caregiver, God is ever present with us. His capacity to be with us in our joys and suffering could not be more absolute: he entered history, lived a life with the full range of human emotions, and died brutally on the cross (Hebrews 4:15). But it may be difficult to experience God being with us if our tendency is to push away particular feelings. The practice of mindful awareness, which encourages us to bring compassion and kindness to that which we find difficult, can "undo the habits of aversion"[9] and may build new muscles for turning to God as both Comforter and Encourager.

Our God-representations

As we practise turning to God in new ways, it may be that this in itself creates an expansion in our heart knowledge of him. If we've previously avoided the practice of being in his presence while at the same time holding an awareness of our guilt, for example, then it may be that a new practice of being intentionally open and offering ourselves unveiled at such times, may help us discover that our turning to him is not what we had feared. If we begin to turn to him as if our head knowledge of God as both Comforter and Encourager is true, then we begin to practise new *attachment behaviours*. When we experience a new reality through new ways of being and relating, then we can strengthen the beliefs that this reality affirms.

Yes... but...

Aren't "images" idols?

Making an image of something and bowing down and worshipping it is idolatry (Isaiah 44); so is mistaking creatures for the Creator (Romans 1:25). We must always guard against this.

But having a mental picture of God is simply the way we respond to God as human beings. The fact that God has provided such a rich number of images for us in Scripture is a measure of his grace in reaching out towards us, and correcting our bad mental pictures.

The great Swiss reformer Jean Calvin puts it this way: "For who even of slight intelligence does not understand that, as nurses commonly do with infants, God is wont in a measure to 'lisp' in speaking to us? Thus such forms of speaking do not so much express clearly what God is like as accommodate the knowledge of him to our slight capacity. To do this he must descend far beneath his loftiness" (*Institutes of the Christian Religion* (1960), ed. J. T. McNeill, tr. F. L. Battles. Philadelphia, PA: Westminster, 1.13.1).

But there is another way that we might enlarge our heart knowledge of God. We can be mindful of how we mentally picture God in our imagination, and cultivate a representation that communicates more fully God's compassion.

Clinical psychologists Paul Gilbert and Ann Hackmann have developed imagery work to help clients enhance their capacity for feelings of affection, warmth, connectedness, and compassion. Similar to the head/heart discrepancy that we can have in relation to our beliefs about God, clients in therapy often find that they *know* something to be true but don't *feel* that it is true. Someone who has been sexually assaulted, for example, might say, "I know that it wasn't my fault but I still *feel* that it was." Deborah Lee uses an approach that involves helping people struggling with shame or excessive self-criticism develop and focus on a representation of a compassionate figure. This does not have to be a human figure, but it does need to capture compassionate qualities including wisdom, strength, warmth, and non-judgment. The representation may be visual, but some people prefer to engage through the sense of touch or hearing. Bringing together multiple senses can be particularly powerful. Pictures often contain more emotional meaning than words, and can therefore help us to have a felt experience of what we previously only knew intellectually. This sort of compassionate imagery has been found to transform self-attacking thoughts, or the toxic meaning carried in hurtful and traumatic memories of the past.

Inspired by the work of these psychologists, and aware of the power of imagery to impact our heart knowledge, some of us have used these methods with Christians in both church and therapeutic contexts. Sometimes this has been a simple exercise of evoking a compassionate picture that communicates at a heart level what we already know in our heads to be true. At other times, clients are asked to bring up a picture that communicates God's perspective to a trauma in the past. The Encounter Course[10] focuses on using experiential exercises to help participants consciously receive God's compassion. As well as exercises that allow participants to practise seeing God as both *Comforter* and *Encourager*, they are also helped to identify limitations in their heart knowledge of God using, among other methods, the "God Image Questionnaire".[11] Participants then prayerfully develop a multisensory picture of God's character that incorporates the qualities that had previously been lacking.

Get Some Exercise!

Developing good God-representations

This exercise works best for a group of people who know each other reasonably well. It may help participants to read this chapter first. The aim is to cultivate God-representations that are true to God's character and communicate compassion.

As a group, list some adjectives to describe God. Ideally those suggested should feel personally relevant.

Take ten minutes individually to allow a multisensory image of God to emerge that communicates these qualities. Think about smells, touch, sound, etc. The image may only be fleeting. That is OK. If unwanted thoughts come or you get distracted, acknowledge where your mind has gone and gently bring yourself back to the task. Before you start, pray that God will be working with you as you imagine.

Take five minutes to meditate on this image. Allow what emerges to interact with you to help you receive God.

Talk about what you noticed as a group. Be open to discussion about any disappointments or frustrations.

Greater awareness of our God-representations gives us clearer sight of them, helping us to discern what aspects of these may be related to memories of past experiences or other people who may have hurt us. For example, Debbie was troubled by the thought that as a Christian she shouldn't be feeling anxious. She noticed that behind this anxiety was a sense of God rolling his eyes at her. As soon as she noticed this mental image, she realized that she was allowing upsetting memories of her father rolling his eyes to distort her relationship with God. This insight freed her to grow in the confidence that this impatient criticism was not coming from God at all.

Our God-representations can also reveal something important about the degree to which we know God as both *Comforter* and *Encourager*. For example, as part of his therapy James pictured God as a warm, glowing, fire. He understood the fire to be encouraging him to "Go, go", just as he was about to embark on a new career. When he returned the following week after a difficult life event, he related to this image very differently. This time he wanted to keep himself away from the fire with a sense of shame. James was very able to know God as his Encourager but less able to come to God with difficult feelings. This reflected his early experience of being supported in career achievements but less so with feelings or behaviours deemed to be unacceptable.

Sometimes intentionally reflecting on the way we imagine God to be addresses a particular need in the moment. Consistent with Paul Gilbert's work, seeing God as Comforter can create feelings of being soothed, safe, connected, and "not wanting". Emily's imaginative experience was of being rocked in a cradle. She said she felt "more relaxed, safer, focused, reassured, hopeful, peaceful, at home, comforted, without loss, satisfied". John had a similar picture of being pushed in a pram and experiencing it as a place of "safety, protection, nurture". Celina found it helpful to bring C. S. Lewis' Aslan[12] to mind. The lion was a reminder of the awe of God: "… the idea of a lion being so close it can lick you … how big a lion's tongue …" For her, the lick of this tongue could bring either healing or hope, depending on the need.

Other pictures have facilitated an understanding of God as Encourager, helping to let go of worry and engage with the world. Fiona was caught up in worry that her toddler hadn't thanked a neighbour for a toy he'd received. The picture that came to her was of a dolphin character from a children's story. This dolphin has a great sense of humour: "He's always laughing. He's always trusting people with really big things and they mess up… There's never any blame." Imagining her son riding on the back of this dolphin put into perspective concern about what others thought and brought into focus God's delight in her son playing.

God-representations and mindfulness

These examples suggest that working with God-related imagery can support the kind of attitude that underpins both mindful awareness and secure attachment. Emily and John's images facilitated closeness and Fiona's image helped her let go of her worry. Sometimes a God-representation can even affirm the mindful practice of being with difficult feelings. For example, Karla had been struggling with a fear about the possibility of a break-in at her home. She would listen out for danger, remembering suspicious characters she had seen in her neighbourhood. She had done some work to experiment with allowing herself to "be with" the fear and, having done this, was encouraged to see what would happen if she brought God to this through imagery. She described the experience as: "I realized that God notices with me and he notices me. I learned that I can just 'notice', without having to problem-solve. As I dwelled on the different things I was noticing (with each of my senses…)

I saw images of God placing his hands tenderly over each of my eyes, ears, and mouth, as if to convey, 'yes, I am noticing that [noise/person/breath] too, and I am here with you in that'. It was powerful for me to experience God 'just noticing' with me, without either of us having to present an explanation. I felt a release in allowing myself to sit and be with God in the middle of feeling afraid."

The process of imagination required when invoking a particular God-representation is often best underpinned by a mindful attitude. It is important not to force things, to remember that mental images come and go, and that it is normal for them to be quite fleeting. If a mental image fades or the mind wanders, it is very important to bring it back *gently*, knowing that wandering is what minds do. It can also be tempting to feel self-critical if no clear God-representation emerges. Again, kindness to self is important here. God-representations may convey truth about who God is and about his compassion for us, but they are only mental tools to help our limited capacities. C. S. Lewis says, "My idea of God is not a divine idea. It has to be shattered time after time. He shatters it Himself. He is the great Iconoclast."[13]

As we "shatter and build time after time", we need to be mindful that there is a "deeper magic",[14] more powerful and more compassionate than our images can ever convey. We rest on metaphors as best we can, assured that the deeper truth is even more delicious than we can possibly know (1 Corinthians 13:12). Perhaps it is less important to keep comparing our heart knowledge with our head knowledge than to know that all of us need continually to return to the source of the river to drink. It is this coming close for healing, restoration, and forgiveness that will enable us to take living water to the world.

When Two or Three are Gathered...

Questions for group discussion

Talk together about your own experiences of God as:

An Encourager

A Comforter

When have you resisted coming to God as Comforter?

Can you recall moments when it has been difficult to joyfully engage with the world or get on with a task because worry has got in the way?

Which Bible stories come to mind that demonstrate God as a Comforter or Encourager?

Courage

Turning Inward with Eyes to See

"We must lay before Him what is in us; not what ought to be in us."[1]

We may have a good image of God. We may have a rich image of God. We may see God as compassionate, wise, powerful, and tender. But we will only dare to turn to him fully if we are brave enough to offer our unveiled selves. Just as Adam and Eve covered themselves in fig leaves to hide from God in their shame (Genesis 3:7), so too do we use psychological fig leaves. We hide from God and ourselves through our attempts to control, suppress, amplify, and fixate on certain aspects of our everyday experience. In situations of crisis when we are desperate we may forget our shame and throw ourselves on God's mercy, but for the most part we are reluctant to "approach the throne of grace" (Hebrews 4:16).

Yet God has dealt with our shame through the life, death, and resurrection of Jesus. We can come to him without hiding (Romans 5:1–2). Mindful habits can help us realize this through the practice of being with our thoughts, feelings, and body sensations just as they are. In the knowledge of God's compassionate presence, we can bring self-compassion to these experiences. Open-hearted, we can also turn to God and know his being with us in all our fear, sin, weakness, and affliction. There's no need to hide.

The place of clear awareness

In this chapter we focus on the capacity to be with our inner experience. When we talk about attention to the self in mindfulness, we are talking about a clear awareness of what is taking place in the moment, whether it be things around us or within us. It is a "pre-reflective" mode which "reveals what is occurring, before or beyond *ideas* about what is or has taken place".[2]

Various metaphors have been used to help us think about the way things are brought into clear awareness in any moment. The psychiatrist Dan Siegel uses a picture of a bicycle wheel with the hub at the centre, and the spokes leading to the rim around the outside. He calls this the "wheel of awareness". From the hub, we attend to whatever it is that we choose to focus on: sensory information in our environment, bodily sensations, or the images, thoughts, or memories that run through our minds. These objects of attention are around the rim of the wheel, and we can choose where on the rim we focus our attention. For example we may focus on the discomfort in our stomach or the light reflections in a body of water, or a memory of saying goodbye. Siegel describes the hub as "a place of tranquillity, of safety, of openness, and curiosity" from which we can "receive any aspect of experience, just as it is".[3]

This practice of awareness from a position of calm, allows us to simply observe what may look like pretty turbulent emotions, thereby giving us perspective and clarity. We may be ruminating about an insensitive remark we made, or worrying about whether we are going to meet a deadline, but noticing the thought churning can be a moment of mindful awareness.

Where Did it Come From?

Thoughts of the heart

In the Christian tradition the practice of being transparent about inward thoughts without being held back by shame was a central principle of the group of people we now call the "desert fathers and mothers". The most famous of these is Antony of Egypt (d. 356).

The desert is a place that strips away all one's attempts at distraction and self-delusion and invites you to face yourself. But you won't get far in dealing with what you find without a wise guide. So, the desert fathers and mothers provided this for others who came to consult them about what they found when they looked inward.

This practice was called "manifesting the thoughts of the heart". The key thing was to get the thoughts and feelings – either sinful or simply distracting – out in the open and own them. This was not so much to confess and seek pardon (as in later medieval Western Christianity), but more to be able to look at the self with "sober judgment" (Romans 12:3) and so develop humility and obedience to the mind of Christ.

John Cassian (360–435) taught that this practice of honest self-examination and revelation to another breaks the hold of shame and nurtures the sort of faith that allows one to accept the grace of God.

It reminds us that this is worry rather than a real impending catastrophe. This awareness gives us a broader perspective and the space to *respond rather than react*. In the words of Kirk Brown and Richard Ryan, "As a form of receptive awareness, mindfulness may facilitate the creation of an interval of time or a gap wherein one is able to view one's mental landscape, including one's behavioural options, rather than simply react to interpersonal events."[4]

You may be thinking that this all sounds fairly straightforward, but there's a reason for the emphasis on "non-judgment" and "acceptance" in mindfulness. It's not just a matter of bringing our distracted minds gently back to our intended focus. There can be powerful pulls away from the tranquil hub and out of the present moment because of particular judgments about what we should or shouldn't be thinking or feeling.

Our view obscured by fear

Often it is fear that obscures our capacity to stay with our experience for long enough to see what is actually present. We have an internal alarm system that is employed to detect threats quickly. As we are wired to prioritize survival, this system can be rather indiscriminate. We can be put on high alert to respond to danger when there is none. This means that people or situations or objects in our environment that bear a resemblance to a previously upsetting event can trigger anxiety unnecessarily.

If I have been witness to domestic violence during childhood, and I find myself in the pub with two friends who raise their voices in a heated political debate, it is possible that this could feel threatening because in the past, raised voices signalled imminent violence. My body may react as if the past danger were in the present. Instead of staying aware of the present moment, I am already searching for a means of escape. The more I notice the facts of the present situation, while aware that my sense of threat is being fuelled by trauma memories, the more I can feel grounded in the present. I can hear that the voices are raised, but notice smiles between comments. I remain aware that I am an adult and not a child. Having recognized that my anxiety is fuelled by terrifying events in the past, I can offer kindness to myself. If I can stay in the situation, it gives me the chance to learn that raised voices don't necessarily signal danger.

Just as a fear of external circumstances can restrict our openness to the present, so too can a fear of our *internal* experience. Many clients come to therapy fearful of their own emotions. Severe anxiety symptoms can be misinterpreted as signalling imminent death from a heart attack; anger can arouse fears of exploding or being violent; allowing oneself to cry can feel like turning on a tap that may never turn off. We may even fear positive emotions such as happiness and compassion. But, like physical pain, emotions are important signals. Trying to suppress an emotion means that we don't allow ourselves to test out what it actually feels like or hear what it is telling us. We never get the chance to see that emotions are time-limited. Like waves our emotions come and go, they rise and fall. Even if our emotions are difficult, we can work through them and get to the other side. When we allow ourselves to feel the emotion, we are in a better position to take effective action or seek appropriate help or support, and are no longer expending energy trying to keep it away.

Hardening of the "oughteries"

Sometimes it is not so much that we are suppressing the emotion but more that we are reacting to it with judgment and criticism. This may be because we are focusing on the gap between how we think we ought to feel and how we actually feel (as when we judge the discrepancy between our head and heart knowledge of God). This can be like heaping coal onto an already burning fire:

> *Sandra was a determined woman in her thirties with
> exceptionally high standards. A venture in which she
> had invested everything had not succeeded, and she was
> experiencing understandable grief. She was someone who*

was very used to approaching challenge and making things happen in the world and at church, but she found it hard to accept and be with her difficult feelings. In response to feeling tearful, instead of simply acknowledging her grief, she would conclude that she was "a wreck" and begin to worry that she would never be able to cope. These thoughts added anxiety and shame to the already painful grief.

Mindfulness can help us be with our emotions rather than suppressing or reacting to them. One simple and effective technique is to talk people through a mindful exercise that helps them notice the sensations in their body that arise as they feel emotion. The person is encouraged to avoid trying to change what she notices, and instead to watch what happens as the sensations change over time. The process of intentionally meeting with those sensations helps to "befriend" them. Somehow, being aware of the physical sensations and holding them in awareness can feel like tending to a physical wound. "When we experience our emotions on the physical level, rather than thinking about what's making us so unhappy, it's easier to stay present […] By staying anchored in our body, we can soothe and comfort ourselves for the pain we're feeling without getting lost in negativity."[5]

What a shame

Get Some Exercise!

The grumpy hedgehog experiment

Briefly imagine a grumpy hedgehog.

For one minute, close your eyes, but make sure you don't allow yourself to think of the grumpy hedgehog.

What did you notice?

Sometimes we push away thoughts or images if we feel ashamed of them. It is pretty common to have all kinds of unpleasant and unwanted intrusive thoughts, like violent or sexual images. This doesn't necessarily mean anything about our character. Thoughts like this can be random aspects of consciousness, but when we give them attention and worry about them we can lend them meaning and significance. In fact, the aversion to the thought, pushing it away, can give rise to more intrusions. This was well recognized by the early Christian desert fathers and mothers who warned novices against trying to suppress impure thoughts and images for this very reason.

Get Some Exercise!

Three-minute mindfulness

Set a timer for three minutes.

Sit in an alert but comfortable position and close your eyes.

Watch the contents of your mind.

When the timer goes off, see if you can write down some examples of what you noticed:

Thoughts (e.g. "what a waste of time", "when is the timer going to go off", etc.)

Images or memories

Feelings (e.g. anger, sadness, joy, tranquillity, boredom, etc.)

Bodily sensations (e.g. a heaviness in our chest, a pain above our eyes).

In one modern study, people who were told to suppress their unwanted thoughts had more frequent thoughts and experienced them with greater discomfort than people who were told to think about or record their thoughts.[6] You can demonstrate this for yourself by having a go at the "Grumpy Hedgehog" exercise in the text box above. You'll see that sometimes simply trying not to think about something can mean that we end up thinking about it more. Part of the rationale of mindfulness is that holding difficult thoughts in mind, rather than dismissing them as unbearable, deprives them of the power to disturb and oppress us.

One of the most difficult things to bring into our awareness is the perception that we have failed to meet our own standards. These could be moral standards, or expectations of ourselves at work or socially. Perhaps we've cheated in an exam, or lost our temper with an elderly relative. Perhaps we sent our boss an intimate email intended for our spouse, or we suddenly gained several pounds in weight. We may be guilty of a really serious offence. Whether the unmet standards are moral, social, or performance-related, the discomfort can be intense, because a sense of failure can so quickly lead to shame. Furthermore, our "inner critic" can add layers to this discomfort with self-attacking inner talk. The motivation for this may vary. In Sandra's case she found it difficult to let go of her self-attacking thoughts because, from her perspective, her inner critic was doing the necessary job of keeping her standards high.

The inner critic may also serve a self-protective function. If we can point out our faults first, then the imagined or real accusers in our lives will have no ammunition. It's as if we're saying, "I got there first, so don't try to tell me anything I don't already know." This isn't real Christian contrition for sin but a clever approximation of it – a kind of mental self-harm that keeps us in control. We issue this kind of pre-emptive strike on ourselves because we have either a punitive mental representation of God, or a shameful representation of self or – most likely – both.

Instead of heaping on shame, we can try to avoid it altogether by veering in the opposite direction and getting into denial. We can blame others or make excuses, convincing ourselves that what we did was the only thing that could have been done under the circumstances. We may even continue to inflict hurt on others. Watching an episode of the TV series *The Apprentice* is a good reminder of the lengths people can go to in order to conceal their shortcomings from others and themselves. Yet if we deny being at fault, we not only fail to learn from our mistakes, but go without the opportunity to seek reparation (1 John 1:8).

Coming to the place of clear awareness, where we see specifically how we have fallen short without heaping on shame, can feel painful but it will not destroy us. It's what Paul describes as seeing oneself with "sober judgment" (Romans 12:3). It may require us to recognize that in particular circumstances, we don't perform as well as we would like, or that our comment was hurtful. It can, however, be incredibly freeing, as Danni discovered:

> *I subconsciously reserved a "pedestal" for people I thought were socially accomplished, genuinely compassionate, and talented in every way – what I wanted to be, but knew I wasn't. When I put someone on my pedestal, I felt quite intimidated and inadequate around them, not to mention jealous – they were what I wanted to be. On the rare times I did put myself on the pedestal I knew I didn't really belong there, and would soon fall off. Talking this through has made me realize that it's not about striving for the pedestal – it's about accepting myself as I am – strengths, weaknesses, fears, and failures. It takes humility to accept, not strive, but it's been incredibly freeing.*

If we can come to God baring our faults and receiving his compassion, allowing him to shine the fierce light of his love on them, then we can truly know grace and forgiveness. When we have not hidden behind pre-emptive exaggeration or denial, but have risked exposing ourselves to God's gaze, we can fully discover what it is to be loved unconditionally. Our natural response will be a desire to change for the better, coming not from fear of being shamed and rejected, but from a realization of the love and grace that we have received (John 1:16). As C. S. Lewis writes, "We are always completely, and therefore equally, known to God... We have unveiled. Not that any veil could have baffled His sight. The change is in us. The passive changes to the active. Instead of merely being known, we show, we tell, we offer ourselves to view."[7] As we begin to unveil ourselves in this way, we give ourselves the opportunity for close connection that enables growth and intimacy with God.

Mindful bodies and embodied minds

Up to this point we have been talking mainly about the mind: emotions, thoughts, and images. But this doesn't mean that we have ignored the body. We noted that a mindful focus on our bodily sensations can free us from enslavement to racing thoughts, and we noted that mindfulness can offer us space for leisurely reflection and response, freeing us from the knee-jerk reactivity of the body.

By the Book

The body in the Bible

In the New Testament the Greek word for body, sōma, is a neutral term for the substance or framework of an object or creature. (This is in contrast to the word for flesh – sarx – which is often used negatively to mean a worldly attitude.)

In Philippians 3:21 Paul talks of our present body as "lowly" but awaiting transformation to become glorious. In 1 Thessalonians 5:23 he talks of the Christian's body as "blameless", and in 1 Corinthians 15:40–44 he explains that everything has a body and that we will continue to have a body after death.

For all the New Testament writers, what we do with our body is really important because we are understood to be bodily creatures whose bodies have been redeemed by a bodily Saviour.

However, there is also a lot of talk about the transformation of the mind (e.g. Romans 12:2), and of course Jesus' own words on integrating thinking and action so as to avoid hypocrisy (e.g. Matthew chapter 6 and 15:7–8).

Science and faith come together here because right from the beginning Christianity understood human beings to be embodied creatures. There is no such thing as disembodied mindfulness. The way that God saved human beings was by becoming embodied – incarnate. Salvation is not a disembodied idea but an enfleshed action: "He himself bore our sins in his body on the cross, so that, free from sins, we might live for righteousness; by his wounds you have been healed" (1 Peter 2:24 NRSV). What's more, Paul teaches that the community of faith is Christ's *body* (e.g. 1 Corinthians 12:27).

Mindfulness enables us to have a different relationship with our body, to witness what it does and attend to what it may be telling us. We shouldn't think that mindful detached observation of the body will split mind and body apart. In the developed West we have *already* become cut off from our bodies, and sadly, from early modern times the churches have not been immune to this.[8] Mindfulness helps us to welcome the body back into our thinking, feeling, and actions.

Jesus himself shows a complete integration of mind and body at key points in his own life and ministry. For example we are told in Matthew's Gospel that, "When Jesus landed and saw a large crowd, he had compassion on them and healed their sick" (Matthew 14:14). He felt compassion for the people, and he healed them. Jesus healed from a position of immeasurable love and care. But the physically embodied nature of his love is emphasized in the Greek word *splagchnizomai* that we translate "to have compassion". This word literally means "of the innards and entrails". The King James Version of the Bible captures this well in Philippians 1:8, where it says "For God is my record, how greatly I long after you all *in the bowels* of Jesus Christ."

When Jesus has compassion he is inwardly moved – *all* of him – into action. There is no sense of dispassionate duty here, not a rational and considered analysis followed by a practical application. Instead there is integrated embodied happening: embodied feelings seize the whole person to energize action at that very moment. We see authentic and credible connection to self and others. Jesus is true to himself, his God, and his mission. His compassion is authentically embodied – it looks and feels genuine and therefore is inspiring (Matthew 7:29).

This authenticity comes from the matching up of Jesus' body with his words. We know from research that our body can say more about our motivation and thoughts than our speech (lie detectors are based on this principle). Although cultural norms, peer pressure, or wishful thinking may lead us to say one thing, it is actually the body that so often gives away our deeper thoughts and feelings, even when we ourselves are not fully aware of them. Hence the onlooker trusts the bodily message and is reassured when it matches the verbal message.

Two ways of knowing

Many languages have two different words for "to know" (for example French has *savoir* and *connaître*). These distinguish knowing about something from the knowledge gained by direct experience of a person or event. Job famously makes the distinction between knowing about God and actually encountering God, describing one as "hearing of" and one as "seeing" (Job 42:5).

Help... I'm a Geek

Further reading in this area

For a pastorally insightful theological exploration of shame, you may like to look at:

Goodliff, P. (2005). *With Unveiled Face: A Pastoral and Theological Exploration of Shame*. London: Darton, Longman & Todd.

The details of the wheel of awareness and the hub and spoke meditation exercise can be found in:

Siegel, D. (2010). *Mindsight. Transform Your Brain with the New Science of Kindness*. Oxford: Oneworld.

The need to develop a compassionate attitude towards oneself and others is explained in detail and given a good scientific rationale in both of the following:

Neff, K. (2011). *Self Compassion. Stop Beating Yourself Up and Leave Insecurity Behind*. London: Hodder & Stoughton.

Gilbert, P. (2010). *The Compassionate Mind*. London: Constable.

Different ways of thinking and knowing based on the hemispheres of the brain are explained in the following entertaining but controversial approach to the subject:

McGilchrist, I. (2009). *The Master and His Emissary: The Divided Brain and the Making of the Western World*. Cambridge: Yale University Press.

A complete list of sources is provided in the reference section at the end of the book.

Like Job, psychologists John Teasdale and Phil Barnard make a similar distinction between what they call "propositional" knowing and "implicational" knowing.[9] Propositional knowing is conscious, rational, easy to express in words – knowing about. Implicational knowing is pre-conscious, intuitive, difficult to express in propositions or to defend rationally but much more like direct knowing. Crucially implicational knowing relies on non-verbal bodily signals that communicate the emotional tone of a situation. It yields the sort of compelling yet tacit knowledge that we feel able to trust. According to Teasdale and Barnard the implicational system is understood to integrate rational knowledge with knowledge that comes from internal body states. We might call this sort of knowledge "gut instinct", and so we return to the vocabulary of innards and bowels.

Paying mindful attention to our bodily state therefore can help us gain deeper awareness of ourselves as embodied creatures. It involves intentionally dwelling in bodily based implicational knowing, without switching too quickly into propositional knowing and reflective thinking. This sort of awareness makes it easier for us to be more authentic: for conscious thought, feeling, and action to work together seamlessly in our lives. We can then be fully responsive in the moment, and be people of integrity.

The wisdom of the body

The stories of John and Geoff show how mindfulness enables this "seeing into the body", through real-life examples. Both had been taught mindfulness as part of their psychological therapy. John used it to find a way into the heart of his depression and to open up a way through it. Geoff used it as a way to achieve inner and outer stillness in the midst of anxiety.

John said that he felt low. He thought that "life is not worth living". Indeed he had attempted to take his own life ten years previously, and the memory of this made him more depressed. As part of his therapy he intentionally chose to feel – really feel – this sadness in his body. His stomach felt heavy and dull. There was change in his breathing – heavy, more laboured, with a sense of oppressive weight on his lungs. And his shoulders felt heavy – "like lead" – with so much loaded on them.

He was surprised that his body showed that it was so sad, indeed depressed; it was both a feeling and a posture. In other words, sadness was not just a "mental state". His sadness had a real bodily presence; his body wanted to recoil from life, as both it and he felt weighed down.

John became even more attentive to his body, entering into the depth of his thoughts, feelings, and somatic sensations. He compassionately accepted what he discovered. He sensed profound shame about his suicide attempt, and he noticed this sense of shame moving into a sense of disgust. He witnessed a sense of strong stirring in his stomach, as if to expel his feelings.

And as he made contact with these sensations of disgust and weight in and on his body, he had a sense of what might be helpful, what might ease the load, or signal a way out. He quietly said, "I need to forgive myself."

He began to weep. And he allowed his thoughts, feelings, and somatic sensations to be – really be – and be surrounded in compassion. There was no denial or avoidance, but instead acknowledgment and engagement. He let the heavy thoughts and feelings go, and as he did so his body gained a sense of lightness, "as if a weight had lifted". He became aware of just how much psychological and physical pain he had been holding onto, as he became aware of an emerging sense of freedom in his muscles. There was a sense of inflation in his body as his muscles enlarged. He noticed his shoulders and stomach expand and breathing became easier. He felt present to himself and the world in a new way, and physically he had a stronger and taller posture. He was, as it were, *raised up*.

Geoff, on the other hand, was lying in an MRI scanner, having been asked to stay completely still for thirty minutes. He was having investigations for cancer. Throughout all of his life he had felt in control: his career, his mind, and his personal relationships. And then he developed cancer. He was at a crossroads, questioning how much control he really had in his life. He developed anxiety and depression.

Geoff was very sceptical and scathing about mindfulness – "No need for such tosh!" – but while in the scanner, he had plenty of time to explore his body and consider the merits of this approach. He was surprised to find that his body yielded information of which he was previously unaware. He began to "see" into his body and noticed the association between somatic sensations, thoughts, feelings, and impulses.

After about three minutes in the scanner Geoff noticed that his body had the urge to shift position and move. He was not sure what this was about – he did not feel particularly uncomfortable. He decided to be mindful of this urge, as he needed to override the natural impulses of his body – movement inside the scanner wasn't possible. Indeed, while his body needed to move, he noticed that he was able to override this by exertion of his own will. After about seven minutes, Geoff could feel that his muscles were becoming strained and tired. He became aware again of his body's natural urge to move and continued to override these impulses. While his body was feeling strained and tired, Geoff also noted that his feelings were paralleling this, his anxiety was rising. He noticed that his thoughts fell into the now familiar pattern of being afraid for his future health and seemingly out of control.

The minutes ticked by seemingly very slowly. After about fifteen minutes Geoff's muscles felt very pained, stretched, and pulled – not surprising after the length of time in the scanner. Geoff noted that he was now very absorbed in overruling his body's natural instincts to shift position. He gained a sense of the location of his body in space, and his levels of muscular tension.

Geoff began to realize that he was able to manage the tension in his muscles with the use of positive and negative words. When he said "No!" he noticed that his muscles felt just a bit tighter, and he himself just a little more tense or anxious. But when he said "Yes!" there was a muscular relaxation and a feeling of psychological and physical relief. It also dawned on him that there was less urge to move when his muscles felt more relaxed. So he alternated between these words and managed to persevere to the end of thirty minutes of immobility. He felt enlightened. He had discovered that by being hospitable to his body he was able to work with it, rather than against it, to achieve his goal of stillness.

This is one of the great benefits of mindfulness for the Christian. We can often be fearful of pausing to look within ourselves. We fear uncovering our sinfulness or our shame. Yet, when we allow God to assist us in mindfully looking within, we allow his grace and forgiveness to reach the deepest parts of our being. When Jesus gives us the eyes to see, we need not fear to look within; we can do so with courage.

When Two or Three are Gathered...

Questions for group discussion

Which inner experiences (thoughts, feelings, bodily sensations) do you dislike? What do you do when these rise up to bother you?

Who can recall a time when they remained calm and still inside, even though life was full of upheaval or stress? Tell the group about what it was like.

What does your inner critic say when it attacks you? What would a more compassionate, encouraging voice say instead?

When have you been inwardly moved with compassion as Jesus was? What happened as a result?

What signals of pleasure or distress has your body given you lately? Is there anything you need to do about them?

Turning Towards Pain and Need

"Good" pain and "bad" pain

In the last few chapters we have covered a lot of ground. We've recognized that we can turn to God as a comforter and an encourager rather than as one who rejects or punishes us. We've looked at turning inwards without shame, exaggeration, or denial, but rather taking an honest view of our inner thoughts, images, and feelings, offering them up unveiled to our compassionate God. We also saw that this is a completely embodied process and that a mindful attitude can help us to receive the wisdom of the body. So far so good.

By the Book

Pain and growth in the Bible

We can be reassured that Jesus knows what real pain is, whatever we are struggling with. He has endured physical and psychological pain, as Isaiah writes of him: "He is despised and rejected of men; a man of sorrows, and acquainted with grief" (Isaiah 53:3 KJV).

Pain produces and matures good and everlasting fruit: perseverance, character, and hope (Romans 5:3–5). Jesus makes it very clear that if fruit does not follow then there is very hard pruning, even complete removal. Discipleship happens through pain – to bear everlasting fruit that is reflective of the kingdom (John 15:2–6).

Whatever happens in life's struggles and pain, Jesus promises that he will be with us (Matthew 28:20). We do not need to feel alone. God's compassion is with us and we can shelter in his covering. In the words of the psalmist, "Surely your goodness and love will follow me all the days of my life, and I will dwell in the house of the Lord forever" (Psalm 23:6).

But what happens when our inner experience is so dominated by pain that we cannot bear to look it in the face? It is the most natural and healthy thing to have physical pain when injured or in childbirth. It is the most natural and healthy thing to have psychological pain such as fear of danger or grief at loss. Pain tells us that something significant is happening. Like healthy emotion, it should be a relatively short-lived signal. But for many people, pain is not short-lived. It becomes a chronic presence in their lives, ceasing to do its work as a signal of significance and simply causing them misery.

Research and clinical experience all show that mindfulness can be a powerful way to break into this misery, opening the door to compassion, release, and strength. There is a view, certainly among clinicians, that those struggling with psychological and/ or physical pain are actually closer to a sense of reality. Even "bad" pain can bring unexpected gifts. The affected person may not be able to articulate this clearly, but mindfulness can be a way of fostering this insight so that life and its struggles can be seen not only *from* a different vantage point but most unexpectedly with different eyes. Looking at pain mindfully can be the choice of a different way of living, resulting in real and measurable change. We need not be afraid of turning towards pain.

Our reactions to pain can make things worse

Anxiety and depression often go together. They are based on healthy emotions that would have been short-lived danger signals in the settings in which we evolved. Nowadays, outside of war zones, most of the dangers that face us are social rather than physical. We don't solve them by rapid-response fight/flight but by more drawn-out strategic and sophisticated social performance. This means that instead of short-lived emotion focused on physical catastrophes, we experience longer-term mood states focused on our position in our social group. We get anxious and depressed if we feel we don't measure up in our group or are in danger of failing and being rejected. These feelings arise from constant social comparison: the urge to judge ourselves against others.

Underpinning this is the fear of non-survival, for if our group rejects us and we find ourselves alone we will indeed be in physical danger. All of us, it is said, are just two steps from homelessness. We are therefore motivated to grasp material things as a form of insurance (Luke 12:16–19) and to achieve a good status in our social group. As a result, a sense of threat from the outside world and negative self-criticism can easily predominate and take over.

Chronic pain is somewhat like anxiety and depression. It is a signal from the body designed to help us, that has gone wrong and is no longer useful. The pain has overstayed its welcome. Chronic pain is defined as pain that lasts longer than three months and that does not arise directly from damaged tissue. There is no straightforward way to treat it and it frequently accompanies conditions such as cancer, fibromyalgia, spinal injury, and arthritis. It's therefore not surprising that people who experience chronic pain very often also display symptoms of anxiety and depression. A sense of hopelessness and helplessness can prevail. There can be a loss of control, dignity, and humanity. An individual can feel like an outsider in society, very alone.

We all constantly face problems, but often a problem can be made worse by our emotional reaction to it. Sometimes this reaction becomes a problem in itself. Often we do more than simply react. We try to cope with the situation by thinking about how we could solve the problem (worrying), or we try to cope with our emotional reaction with psychological strategies like avoidance, distraction, or denial. But these strategies may not improve our mood. Especially with irreversible problems such as bereavement, disability, or long-term health conditions, the psychological strategies often only work in the short term by putting a lid on our feelings. And yet we so often persist with these strategies, even when we know in our hearts that they don't deliver the serenity we are looking for.

Some of us have worked clinically with people who are stuck in unhelpful reactions like this. They have become trapped in their own attempts to cope. They talk of life simply as existence – as "death warmed up". There is no sense of somatic feeling, thoughts of achievement, meaning, or life purpose – there is a lack of energy or engagement with life. There is a sense that for them "life has been laid down"; they have no sense of influence or control over their lives. They do not feel alive.

This is the opposite of Jesus' statement that he has authority to lay down and take up life: "No one takes it [life] from me, but I lay it down of my own accord. I have authority to lay it down and authority to take it up again. This command I received from my Father" (John 10:18). Jesus had a life which he chose to live sacrificially and then to lay down sacrificially. These people feel they have no real life. Yet Jesus' statement invites us to think about how they might, by aligning themselves with him, take up their lives and live them to the full (John 10:10).

Get Some Exercise!

Mindful body scan

One of the most popular introductory exercises for beginners in mindful practice has been alluded to in previous chapters: the mindful body scan. It is for anyone to practise, but is especially helpful to people who experience bodily discomfort. It is a simple exercise, similar to some of the practices mentioned in this chapter, that allows an accepting, non-judgmental awareness of the body and physical sensation. You can give it a go by following these simple instructions:

Sit comfortably in a position that you will be able to maintain for ten minutes or so. This usually means uncrossed legs, upright posture, feet flat on the floor, and hands resting on your lap or the arms of the chair.

Close your eyes and direct your attention to the top of your head. Notice any impulses, sensations, or changes in temperature that occur in that part of the body. After a few moments, move the spotlight of your attention down the body to the following areas, pausing for a minute or two on each:

Face	Neck
Shoulders	Arms
Wrists	Hands
Chest	Stomach
Pelvis	Thighs
Knees	Lower legs
Ankles	Feet

Focus on each area with curiosity concerning what you are likely to find there. As you do, thoughts, images, and judgments are bound to arise. As you notice these, gently return your attention to the part of the body you are currently holding in awareness.

When you have scanned through your whole body, before moving, notice how you feel different and reflect upon what you have learned through kindly awareness of the body.

We have been made in the image of God (Genesis 1:26–27). We can retrieve this life of God embodied within us. This gift of embodiment is astounding. Our body knows how to grieve, enjoy, work, achieve, heal, and connect with others. Living life to the full begins with receiving the wisdom of our God-given body. But where there is physical and psychological pain there is fragmentation, and receiving the wisdom of the body seems to be beyond us. This is where mindfulness can help. It cannot replace the work of the Spirit, but it can enable us to be more in tune with ourselves and so free us to be more open to God.

A real life example: "James"

The story of James illustrates the potential benefits of mindfulness for people who face chronic pain and psychological turmoil. He had been experiencing a chronic health condition for fifteen years. It was very debilitating. Every day he felt widespread pain throughout his body. He was taking the full dose and range of medication prescribed by his consultant. He felt completely exhausted all the time, as if he had flu. Everyday tasks were burdensome, even maintaining the house was impossible at times. He was unable to hold down a job as his health was unreliable. There were days when he did not do anything at all. He felt he was letting everyone down, particularly his wife and two children.

Understandably James experienced symptoms of anxiety and depression alongside his physical symptoms. He was afraid for the future: his health, his finances, and his family responsibilities. He felt ashamed of himself and the distress he was causing his family. He felt that he was just a burden, unworthy, and that life was just an existence without meaning or purpose.

In spite of all this pain and turmoil, however, James really engaged with mindfulness. He found great benefit in exercises that encouraged him to take a non-judgmental, compassionate view of his physical and psychological pain. In one particular session he expressed acceptance of himself. He said that he had never felt such an explosive force of compassionate energy emanate from himself. He no longer felt the need to be self-critical, or strive to understand and escape from his inner confusion. He just accepted it. He had turned and moved towards his pain. The shame and sense of indignity he had been trying to run away from for such a long time no longer scared him.

From his perspective the biggest surprise was his ability to feel compassion and acceptance in his body. This brought him a sense of stillness, a gentle calm, and a real warmth, particularly around his chest area. He noticed his thoughts, which now included the quiet belief that he was worthy of compassion. He realized that anxious and depressive thoughts could be just noticed without having to react to them. And frequently, as a result, these thoughts softened and melted away. He described making contact with his "true self" and life values. The care and nurturance of his family, a sense of adventure, and creativity were central to who he was. He became aware of what these values felt like in his body, their warmth, excitement, and energy.

Mindfulness allowed James to look at his life from a different vantage point. Thoughts, bodily sensations, and emotions could be viewed as *just* events which he simply chose to witness. He was not embroiled in them, nor required to act as referee between them. He became a gentle, compassionate observer of himself.

Shortly after this particular session, James noted that his sense of physical pain had lessened and furthermore that he no longer needed the same amount of medication. James continued to practise mindfulness exercises at home as well as in therapy, and his anxiety and depression symptoms fell below the clinically significant level. His family relationships improved, and he took on part-time voluntary work with a view to future paid employment. Mindfulness had enabled a different relationship with thoughts, somatic sensations, feelings, and behavioural responses. James was able to get on with his life.

Living life to the full

Fundamentally, in Jesus, God himself turns towards human pain and struggle. He draws close to his creation, and enters into it. The shame and indignity of the oppressed were of central concern for Jesus. He worked out of compassion towards the burdened, and indignation towards those who abused power (e.g. Mark 7:6–13). He offered healing as a way through or out of struggles, and often commanded the healed to "Go" or "Go in peace" – literally "Get on with your life" (e.g. Mark 5:19, 34; Luke 7:50; John 8:11).

Jesus embraced his own embodiment, including both psychological and physical pain. In Gethsemane we are told of his bodily agony and turmoil: "And being in anguish, he prayed more earnestly, and his sweat was like drops of blood falling to the ground" (Luke 22:44). The bodily violation of his subsequent crucifixion exemplifies a deep fragmentation – alienation from humankind and separation from his Father (Matthew 27:46). There is a full embrace of shame, indignity, and rejection. Jesus knows what pain is. He has been there too (Hebrews 2:17–18).

Help... I'm a Geek

Further reading in this area

If you would like to read more on the way in which bodily awareness is related to healing and therapy, we would recommend:

Rothschild, B. (2000). *The Body Remembers: The Psychophysiology of Trauma and Trauma Treatment.* New York: Norton Professional Books.

Similarly, Acceptance and Commitment Therapy (ACT) is mentioned several times in this chapter. For a beginner's guide you could look at the following:

Harris, R. (2009). *ACT Made Simple.* Oakland, CA: New Harbinger.

For further details of the Christian approach to mindfulness referenced here, you can turn to:

Symington, S. H. & Symington, M. F. (2012) A Christian model of mindfulness: Using mindfulness principles to support psychological well-being, value-based behaviour, and the Christian spiritual journey. *Journal of Psychology and Christianity* 31(1), pages 71–77.

A complete list of sources is provided in the reference section at the end of the book.

But life is taken up again by Christ and, like the paralysed man who was asked to take up his bed and walk, we too are invited to take up and get on with our lives. This is a form of witness, living in mindful awareness of the incarnate God who willingly turned towards and suffered the depths of human pain. This God continues to be present with us in our suffering.

For any person in pain the practice of mindfulness is likely to be helpful. Turning towards our pain with a detached hospitality can bring perspective and stillness. But for the Christian, who understands God's presence in our pain, there will be a sense of not being in this place alone. Furthermore, the practice of mindful acceptance of pain may paradoxically open a door to

God's work of re-creation in our lives by letting us "be" (after Matthew 16:25).

Mindfulness and being

Taken as a whole, mindfulness is a gentle tool for learning to be. When mindful we can see the gift of grace, compassion, and acceptance from a gentle and quiet base. There is acknowledgment, holding, and validation of our moment-by-moment experience. All of this stands in stark opposition to many of the values of the developed world, with its top-down pressure and striving; its tendency to measure, judge, and dismiss that which has no immediate use. Our society tends to treat individuals as instances of the general rather than as unique persons.

Focus on the individual is paramount in mindfulness, especially when used as part of a clinical approach such as Acceptance and Commitment Therapy (ACT).[1] It is personalized, capable of acknowledging the individual worth of a person. The sheer value of an individual surpasses any angle of the "utility" of that person. This can give confidence in being, and a confidence in having a worthy presence. There can be a new-found sense of control and responsibility. There can be a feeling of comfortable liberation from the internalized society rules and a new-found sense of self. Self-consciousness is diminished. Dignity and a sense of personhood can be found or restored.

Faithfulness to "self" and values can be enabled. And with this connection to self, there comes a greater connection with others, especially where previously there were difficult relationships. The re-engagement, compassion, and acceptance of the self overflow, as we start to turn outwards in compassion and acceptance of others.

Good soil for other-centred action

The practice of mindfulness can prepare good soil that is compassionate, attentive, and aware of others. The neuroscientific evidence gathered through brain-imaging studies suggests that the structure and activity of the brain change for the better through mindful practices.[2] It is consistently recorded that people become more compassionate, empathic, relational, and less fearful through mindful awareness or meditative practices.[3] There are specific compassion meditations that are used in mindfulness training that help facilitate this, although work on compassion could also be seen as a separate and overlapping development within secular psychology.[4] Mindfulness, it seems, moves us from closed and fearful states of mind, to more open states of mind, where a wider range of responses, rather than fearful, automatic reactions, are available to us – perhaps including active concern for others.

Nevertheless, one of the critiques of secular mindfulness is that it is individualistic and narrow in its concerns. This is a legitimate concern but there is evidence that mindfulness can be used to help people access their values and put them into practice when incorporated into a framework that emphasizes this. ACT is a mindfulness-incorporating therapy, and recognizes that people have values that are important to them, but don't necessarily have them in conscious awareness as they live their lives. ACT helps people work with their values as part of the therapy. ACT defines values as something you put into action, not just something you hold as an ideal but do nothing with.[5]

Symington and Symington have developed a Christian approach that uses mindfulness to help clients (who are Christians) become aware of their values and live them out more intentionally.[6] These values, which are often biblical in origin, might include turning towards a world in need – a value which many people who are not Christians would also hold within their own ethical stance.

Daniel Siegel as an interpersonal neurobiologist posits eight senses, and the eighth one is a relational sense.[7] As this is cultivated we can become more attuned to others, and this is part of the good soil that mindfulness practice can cultivate – out of which can come a turning towards a world in need. When we are caught up in fearful and automatic patterns of being and doing, a lot of energy is drawn into maintaining this stressed space within. As mindfulness shifts us out of self-preoccupied anxiety, energy is freed up that can be directed elsewhere – including others in need.

But cultivating good soil is not the same as turning towards a world in need. This comes from a clearly articulated intention to do just that. Traditionally this would be rooted in a religious world view – although there are ethics of compassion within secular positions too.

Turning bare attention into attentiveness

How as Christians might we use mindfulness to turn towards a world in need? To answer this question we can focus on an encounter between Peter and Jesus in Mark's Gospel. Three times in Mark, Jesus predicts his suffering and death on a cross and his rising to life again. Each time the disciples reject this and are guilty of experiential avoidance. They won't hear what they don't want to hear. They want a different messiah who is not the suffering servant turned towards others, but a triumphant king who drives the occupying Romans out of the land.

The first time Jesus predicts his suffering and death in Mark chapter 8, we read that Peter takes him aside and rebukes him.

Jesus' reply in verse 33 is very important: "But when Jesus turned and looked at his disciples, he rebuked Peter. 'Get behind me Satan!' he said. 'You do not have in mind the concerns of God, but merely human concerns.'" This is a moment of trial and testing for Jesus and Peter, an ethical moment of choice. Does Jesus move away from his self-understanding as the man for others in a needy world and embrace a more popular path – does Peter give up his fearful saving of self to become a man for others in a needy world?

We all have ethical moments of choice and in them Jesus tells us that our normal fallen way of thinking does not automatically have the things of God in mind, but only selfish human concerns. The clear implication is that we can cultivate a state of mind where we remember the things of God in the ethical moment of choice and act on that. In fact the NKJV translation of Mark 8:33 says this: "'Get behind Me, Satan! For you are not *mindful* of the things of God, but the things of men.'"[8]

What are the things of God in Mark's Gospel? There are many, but here we will focus on one main concern, which is at the heart of turning to a world in need. In Mark 10:45 Jesus defines his mission in the world: "For even the Son of Man did not come to be served, but to serve, and to give his life as a ransom for many." His whole ministry is summarized in this verse, as a turning to a world in need. The disciples are called to follow him in such a ministry.

So how do we begin to remember this ethical, relational, and personal stance in each moment of ethical choice? Jesus models this for us in his consistently making time for silence and solitude away from the calls of the world (Mark 1:35–39). In fact in this passage at the beginning of Mark the disciples hunt him down, and tell him "Everyone is looking for you!" (Mark 1:37). Jesus replies in the ethical moment of choice, "Let us go somewhere else …" (Mark 1:38). The human desire to please people, or to do as the crowds desire, is resisted in the ethical moment of choice, and Jesus chooses the thing of God for that moment.

Historically, Christian contemplative practice is based on Jesus' forty days in the wilderness, his habits of silence and solitude, and meditating on Scripture (which he can remember in the confrontation with Satan in the wilderness (Luke 4:1–13)). These spiritual disciplines help us master our afflictive thoughts, those human things jostling for our attention, which traditionally include pride, sadness, lust, greed, spiritual apathy, and so on. Learning to hold these afflictive thoughts, rather than being held by them, enabled the early Christian contemplatives to do what God wanted them to do, even in the midst of test, trial, and temptation. They were deeply psychologically informed. There is much overlap between their practices and secular psychology today. But distinctively these early contemplatives, as modelled by Jesus, were developing an other-focused attentiveness out of their God-given capacity for attention and awareness.

Living in a transparent house

Mindful awareness can create the good soil that allows us to consider turning towards a world in need. One of the best metaphors on this comes from Ellen Langer; she likens living in a mindful state of mind to "living in a transparent house".[9] What she means is that more things now stand out for us in our awareness. She says, "In the houses in which most of us now live, if we were in the living room and needed an object (idea) that was in the basement, we might not be aware of its presence. But in our transparent house, objects would be ever available. When in the living room, we could still see the object in the basement even if we chose not to think about it or use it at the moment."[10]

Let's say that the object in question is a value that says, "turn towards the world in need" – there still needs to be an intention to act on that value. Like Jesus, it would involve cultivating states of mind where we mindfully remember the things of God in each ethical moment of choice, where we notice the automatic human reactions jostling strongly for our attention, but still choose the things of God. Bare attention needs to become personal, relational, and ethical attentiveness – which is the intention of spiritual formation within Christianity.

When Two or Three are Gathered...

Questions for small group discussion

You may like to use the following questions to discuss the chapter as a small group.

Do you think God is with you, or possibly abandoned you, when you experience pain (psychological or physical)?

How strange is it to engage and walk towards the pain (psychological or physical)? Is it more comfortable to avoid or deny it?

What do you think about the view that mindfulness is one of the many points where God meets with us in our struggling and suffering?

When has your own pain turned you outwards in an appreciation of the needs of others?

Curiosity

Mindful Bible Reading

Mindful colouring

You have probably gathered by now that we can be mindful anywhere, doing pretty much anything. It takes very little effort at any point in the day to switch off autopilot and direct awareness towards what we are doing, thinking, or feeling. It is this tremendous flexibility in mindfulness practice that has led to the application of mindfulness to a range of activities we might otherwise struggle to view mindfully. Mindful running, mindful kite-flying, mindful calligraphy, mindful knitting... the list is endless. But perhaps one of the most curious applications of mindfulness is found in the recent vogue of mindful colouring books.[1]

Colouring. An activity previously viewed as a rainy day occupation for bored children has suddenly become a therapeutic activity for mature adults. The rationale is pretty much the same as the rationale behind other mindful activities. One can bring mindful awareness to any activity requiring manual dexterity, like colouring. Anything that involves fine motor skills can be used as a focus for mindful attention. Instead of concentrating on the breath, as in more traditional mindful practices, one uses colouring as the focus to which one returns over and over again whenever distractions occur. In the case of mindful colouring, the activity is relatively easy, but nevertheless requires concentration. Mindful colouring involves suspending self-critical thoughts about our artistic ability, while attending to every stroke of the felt-tip and the nuance of the colours.

Mindful colouring books may strike us as a strangely childish occupation, easily dismissed as a silly distraction from a stressful life. But applying mindfulness to artistic activity has a long history, stretching right back to the mindful calligraphy of Japanese Buddhism or the tradition of Tibetan sand art. A similar logic also underpinned the illuminated gospel manuscripts of the high medieval period, like the Lindisfarne Gospels or the Book of Kells. Prior to the printing press, it was a monastic practice to take time copying the words of Scripture, encircling them with elegant patterns in the most expensive inks available. In doing so, writing became a spiritual discipline, a full immersion in the beauty of the Scripture, a time to contemplate and elaborate the meaning of what had been written.

It wasn't always a perfect practice of course. Sometimes the monks indulged in whimsical doodling in the margins of the scripts. But the aim was to allow themselves to enter a state receptive to what they were writing. Illuminated writing not only illuminated the page with colour but also the writer's mind with Scripture. It terms of the attention involved, it was a mindful activity – a putting aside of all distraction and temptation in the contemplation of the words of Scripture.

Mindful copying

Get Some Exercise!

Beginner's Bible

This exercise is designed to allow you to approach the Bible with a beginner's mind, to see familiar passages as if for the first time.

Take a well-known passage of Scripture and memorize it. For example, you might take Jeremiah 29:11: "'For I know the plans I have for you,' declares the Lord, 'plans to prosper you and not to harm you, plans to give you hope and a future.'"

If you don't know the background or the context of the verse, you may wish to look it up in a Bible commentary, so you understand the meaning of what you are reflecting upon.

Bring the verse to mind, repeat it to yourself, silently and out loud, offer it as a prayer to God, repeat it quickly and slowly, until you are used to chewing it over.

Reflect on it at different times. Try different environments: indoors and outdoors, alone and with others, sitting still or on the move, morning or evening. Try different emotional states: bring it to mind when at peace or in turmoil, satisfied or angry, determined or scared. Notice the different nuances available to you at different times and places.

Even if you are familiar with the passage, imagine what it would be like if you didn't know how it would end; repeat it to yourself word by word as if you don't know what the next word will be. Or imagine how different the meaning would be if you replaced some words with their opposites (e.g. in Jeremiah 29, imagining that the words harm and prosper were switched with each other, allows us to be surprised again by the goodness of God).

After a week or so meditating like this, spend some time journaling your thoughts.

Reading the Bible is one area of Christian living where mindful-like attention can therefore be very helpful, particularly if we are reading the Bible as a devotional or prayerful activity. Interestingly, the Bible itself has quite a bit to say on how it is to be read. Various passages in the Old and New Testaments tell us that the Word of God as preserved in Scripture is not to be glanced over briefly like a trashy novel, or ticked off on the to-do list of a daily study chart. The Bible is to be considered, pondered, and inwardly digested. If prayer is like spiritual breath, then reading the Bible is spiritual food.

This attitude of devotion to the Bible is evident in Jesus. Some scholars have speculated that the book of Deuteronomy was Jesus' favourite book in the Hebrew canon. Not only is it referenced, or at least implied, frequently in the New Testament, but it is the words of Deuteronomy that we find on the lips of Jesus during his temptation in the wilderness. Three times he responds to insidious satanic temptation with words from Deuteronomy. When it came to the crunch, these were the words Jesus reached for to resist the derailment of his ministry.

When asked to identify the greatest commandment, Jesus turns like all good Jews to the sixth chapter of Deuteronomy. The people of Israel were to love the Lord their God with all their hearts, souls, and strength. It is an instruction immediately followed by the requirement to immerse themselves entirely in the laws outlining the way of life God intended for them. Their love for God was to be maintained by their knowledge of his word.

In terms of reading the Bible, therefore, it is in Deuteronomy that we first find practical instruction for leaders of the Jewish nation. Following coronation, a new king was to take the time to write out the entire book of the Law – probably the whole of Deuteronomy rather than the entire Torah. And while we have no biblical record of any Jewish king having performed this, it could be that the rediscovery of this practice is what lay behind the religious reforms during the reign of Josiah (1 Kings 23:19–24). It should be remembered that writing was an advanced technology in the ancient world, not many people could do it, and the process was costly and time-consuming. The instruction in Deuteronomy is therefore suggesting that new rulers take significant time and expense to learn line by line the demands of the Jewish law. They were to dedicate concentration and attention to the commands of God as a way of absorbing them into their being.

In less elaborate ways, therefore, the practice imposed on Jewish kings can be equally fruitful for contemporary Christians. Setting aside time over weeks or even months to write or type out some part of the Bible can bring the Bible to life for us. Mindfully copying, for example, every verse of John's Gospel, while spotting distracting thoughts, and returning gently time and again to a concentration on the text, can be a revelation. Studying the Bible by copying it like this is not only a restful activity, but it allows us to slow down and more deeply consider what is written. Instead of rushing to complete the task, we can dwell on the meaning of the words, allow them to take up more space and forge more connections in our minds. We can note more easily our reactions to what we study. A passage may give us peace, or lead to a sense of repulsion or anger. We may sense the love of God or some fear towards him. All of these responses can be taken in prayer to the living God. Even if we find the passage confusing, we can note our confusion without rushing for an explanation or an immediate answer. Allowing the Bible to confuse us can be valuable if in time it leads to deeper insight.

Mindful writing like this gives God time to speak to us through the word and gives us time to hear and respond to the call we receive. As we reproduce God's word on the page or on a computer screen, the word reproduces in us. Copying text like this can be a really effective means of getting to grips with material that really matters. We write roughly seven times slower than we speak, so taking time to write out the words of Scripture is a good way of giving space and time to allow it to sink into our minds.[2] Writing has also been shown in numerous studies to reduce negative emotion and allow us to savour positive events. Writing can give us a clear mind. It is a practice that deserves attention.

Overcoming bias

Deliberately engaging with the Bible in this mindful way goes some way to helping us overcome the dangers inherent in Bible study. One of these is the tendency to look for a reflection of ourselves in Scripture. If we are not careful, instead of approaching what we read with an open mind and a receptive heart, we can end up poring over the Bible, looking to confirm our previously held opinions. Instead of allowing it to challenge us and sometimes change our minds, we can expect it to endorse all our intentions and plans. Psychologists call this "confirmation bias":[3] our tendency as human beings to ignore evidence that contradicts our cherished assumptions and seek that which supports the opinions we already hold. It can really get in the way of allowing the Bible to speak to us.

This accusation has been thrown at Christians by sceptics and atheists for some time. The Bible, it is argued, is such a wide-ranging anthology of literature that it can be made to say whatever we want it to say. Retreating to study Scripture in isolation therefore never really challenges or changes anyone, it just confirms what they already believe. The Bible, according to this view, leaves some of our most prejudiced and toxic attitudes untouched. This is the assumption that lies behind Bertrand Russell's famous statement that religion makes good men better and bad men worse.

In approaching the Bible though, most genuine Christians would hope for something better than this. Rather than merely confirming and justifying previously held notions, we would hope that reading the Bible could in some way be a formative, or even transformative, experience. It should change us for the better. It should fashion our characters and transform our minds. An authentic engagement with the Bible should not just leave us as we are, or strengthen our less desirable traits. We should experience, to some extent, an inner reformation as we read.

The question therefore is not so much, does reading the Bible make us better people? But rather, *how* should we read the Bible to become better people? This is where a mindful approach could help us. Spotting and suspending previous judgments as we study the Bible can allow us to see new things, to be spoken to afresh, to be challenged and changed at the deepest level. But how does this work?

Rumination

I once read the following message on a church billboard: YOU AREN'T WHAT YOU THINK YOU ARE; BUT WHAT YOU THINK, YOU ARE. Aside from being an object lesson in how punctuation can change the meaning of a phrase, it points to a deep psychological truth. The things that we think about a lot shape our experience. Indeed the thoughts that rattle through our minds on a regular basis come to define us. Who we are is deeply linked with what we think about.

Clinical psychologists use the word "rumination"[4] to describe times when we dwell on our thoughts. Depressed people for example often spend time absorbed in thoughts about how worthless, unlovable, and useless they are. Their minds are filled with painful recollections of the past, dire predictions of the future, and defeatist interpretations of the present. If you have ever been depressed, or know someone who has, you will be familiar with this dark cycle of recurrent negative thinking. This black stream of consciousness makes life unbearable – what we spend time ruminating about has an enormous impact on our psychological and physical health.

This is one of the areas where mindful practice has been found to be most effective in clinical practice. It is particularly helpful for people with recurrent depression, those in the terrible position of dipping in and out of depression numerous times over the course of their adult lives. Mindfulness helps in numerous ways with this condition, but it seems to be particularly useful in preventing the explosion of negative rumination that accompanies the depressed state.[5]

You must have encountered this chain reaction of negative thinking at some point. It goes something like this. You have a thought that makes you scared or sad. This quickly leads to other frightened or saddening thoughts. These thoughts multiply and escalate quickly like bees swarming. And, before you know it, you've worked yourself up into a panic or down into a slump.

Thankfully most of us snap out of this sooner or later. We are distracted or comforted and we move on. But some people don't – and that's what causes significant problems for them. It's also where mindfulness can be very effective. Instead of accepting or even resisting each thought that comes our way, mindfulness allows us to simply observe it, note it, and in doing so find that rather than generating further similarly negative thoughts, the thoughts run into the sand.[6] Somehow noting them as thoughts, without doing anything about them, strips them of the energy to reproduce themselves, and allows the distressing vortex of negative thinking to finally settle.

The point is that mindfulness is not just a way of holding some things attentively in mind, but also a way of letting go of others. In the case of reading the Bible this means allowing the word of God to fill our consciousness while ignoring other interfering thoughts. It's the psychological equivalent of planting and watering a healthy sapling, while leaving the weeds that would otherwise choke it to wither and die. Considering, for example, the words of Jesus carefully means allowing his words to take up residence in places that were previously occupied by much less helpful thinking. It's a reorientation of our mind towards his. This is what the practice of biblical meditation affords us.

Biblical meditation

This is one of the areas where some people would prefer to draw a strict dividing line between mindfulness and meditation. Biblical meditation finds its origin in several passages in the Old and New Testaments where people are advised to give time and attention to divine precepts or sayings. One prominent example would be the words that are spoken to Joshua prior to entering the Promised Land:

> *"Keep this Book of the Law always on your lips; meditate on it day and night, so that you may be careful to do everything written in it. Then you will be prosperous and successful. Have I not commanded you? Be strong and courageous. Do not be afraid; do not be discouraged, for the Lord your God will be with you wherever you go."* (Joshua 1:8–9)

Help... I'm a Geek

Further reading in this area

On bias in reading the Bible see:

Watts, F. (ed.). (2007). *Jesus and Psychology*. London: Darton, Longman & Todd.

On *Lectio Divina* and mindful reading more generally:

Painter, C. V. (2012). *Lectio Divina: The Sacred Art*. London: SPCK.

De Waal, E. (2012). *Lost in Wonder: Rediscovering the Spiritual Art of Attentiveness*. London: Canterbury Press.

A good introduction to Benedictine spirituality:

De Waal, E. (1999). *Seeking God: The Way of St. Benedict*. London: Canterbury Press.

Classics on the Quiet Time:

Graham, B. (2006). *The Journey: How to Live by Faith in an Uncertain World*. Nashville, TN: Nelson.

Tozer, A. W. (1948). *The Pursuit of God*. London: Lakeland.

A complete list of sources is provided in the reference section at the end of the book.

He is told to "meditate" (*hāgâ*) on the Law, day and night, to ensure obedience, prosperity, success, and strength in pursuing the promise that God has made to him and his people. The word meditate here could be understood as "ruminate" – to chew the cud as cows do. It implies bringing Scripture to mind and chewing it over, to reflect on and inwardly digest it. When we digest food, we break it down into nutrients which enter the body and become part of our physical structure. Similarly biblical meditation implies mentally chewing on Scripture until it becomes part of who we are, part of our psychological structure. It's a way of reading the Bible that can genuinely change us.

Mindful Bible reading

In Mark's Gospel, when Jesus was asked to explain his parables, he gave the disciples some advice on how to get to grips with what he was saying:

> *"Consider carefully what you hear… With the measure you use, it will be measured to you – and even more. Whoever has will be given more; whoever does not have, even what they have will be taken from them." (Mark 4:24–25)*

Where Did it Come From?

Lectio Divina

Lectio Divina is most closely associated with Benedict of Nursia (c.480–c.545) though it was further developed in the twelfth century. Benedict founded twelve monasteries near Rome, and finally his most famous monastery at Monte Cassino, between Rome and Naples. Their success seemed to depend on his personal qualities but also the "Rule" which he wrote to govern life in these communities. Mindful reading of the Bible both individually and corporately – what he calls "listening with the heart" – is a key part of this Rule, and the Benedictine order has always placed a strong emphasis on Scripture.

The first Archbishop of Canterbury, Augustine, was a Benedictine monk, and the regular pattern of morning and evening prayer that he established in the English church owes much to the idea of *Lectio Divina*. When in the sixteenth century the English Book of Common Prayer was composed by Thomas Cranmer and others, they continued this tradition. This is why there are daily set readings from the Old and New Testament and such a strong emphasis on reciting the psalms in the Book of Common Prayer and its modern version *Common Worship*.

The Quiet Time is a more recent development, emerging in the first half of the twentieth century but with roots further back in the practice of personal piety of Protestant immigrants to North America. It was in part a reaction to the "muscular" Christianity of the late nineteenth century that had been very focused on intercession and spiritual warfare. The Quiet Time, in contrast, promotes contemplative prayer with the Bible open before one, trusting God to reveal himself in Scripture through his Spirit. Some key proponents were Billy Graham (b.1918), Watchman Nee (1903–1972), and A. W. Tozer (1897–1963).

Jesus tells them to consider his words carefully, and suggests a direct relationship between how much time and attention they give to pondering his words, and how much insight and understanding they are likely to get out of them. One of the reasons his disciples struggled to understand what he was saying is that it ran so counter to what they assumed to be true. Coming to a place of understanding would require them to put their most cherished notions to one side in order to get a clear look at what he was getting at. The revelation they were seeking required a willingness to set aside previous assumptions. This is what Jesus recommended to them and in a sense it is what mindful Bible reading can do for us.

The mindful approach to Scripture that originated in Judaism and was promoted by Jesus was continued by the first Christians in a practice that became known as *Lectio Divina* ("divine reading"). This has remained a popular practice with both individuals and groups up until this day. There are a number of ways of doing it but it is usually divided into four steps: reading the passage (several times), "meditation" (chewing it over), prayer for guidance by the Spirit, and "contemplation". In Latin these stages are *lectio, meditatio, oratio,* and *contemplatio.* It is in the final stage of contemplation that a properly mindful approach is introduced. Our usual assumptions about what the passage means are intentionally suspended and the text is contemplated with a kindly curiosity that does not privilege any particular part. Attention eventually will come to rest on a phrase which does not have to be analysed, but can instead be received as a gift and treasured. This can lead to a new sense of the presence of God in unexpected parts of the text, new depths of meaning, and a new way of seeing life.

Evangelical Christians are more likely to be familiar with the "Quiet Time" than with *Lectio Divina*, but they are in fact very similar to each other. Both place an emphasis on stilling of body and mind; the setting aside of mental agendas that have been described as "the opaque veil that hides the face of God"; reading and ruminating on Scripture; prayerful expectation; and the contemplation of Scripture. The main difference is that the Quiet Time is an individual practice but *Lectio Divina* can be done as a group.

Fast psalms

Doing things mindfully however doesn't always mean doing them slowly. I learned this the hard way. A few years ago I spent a week or so practising mindful walking, intentionally bringing my awareness to each step. Noticing the sensations of flexing and contracting of my muscles as I walked. To do this well, or so I thought, I needed to walk slowly – *very* slowly. So slow in fact that I was barely moving. It was as if someone had pressed a pause button mid-step. Unfortunately I didn't choose the location for my exercise very well, and suddenly realized that walking past shop windows on the high street in slow motion probably looked pretty strange to the shopkeepers who were staring out at me. I was mindful of being embarrassed, and speeded up.

These days I realize that I don't need to walk slowly to be mindful. My feet can move as quickly as they like and my mind can still be aware of the changes in the body that go with the movement. The same goes for Bible reading. We don't have to read the Bible slowly to read it mindfully.

This is what the desert fathers used to do when they prayed through the psalms. Instead of reading them slowly they would pray them to God quickly and passionately, attending not to the content but to the spiritual effect of doing so. Sometimes when we clean or polish a surface we do so quickly, not because we are in a hurry to get through with it, but because we like valuable things to retain their shine. Similarly we can pray the psalms in quick succession, not just to race through them, but to clean, cleanse, and saturate the mind with them. When praying the psalms like this, we don't analyse or ponder them, we simply attend to the purifying spiritual effect gained by praying our way through them at high tempo. We can read through the Bible quickly and yet still be mindfully aware of the overall impression it leaves on us.

There are many ways of reading the Bible mindfully. We have only covered a few of them here. We can read it slowly or quickly, we can chew it over in meditation or live it out in *Lectio Divina*. The main thing that all these approaches hold in common is the intention to allow the word of God to take root in our hearts and influence us deeply. Ultimately, to read the Bible mindfully is to allow the Bible to change our minds.

When Two or Three are Gathered...

Questions for small group discussion

When have you received insight or revelation from God when reading the Bible? What was the insight? How were you reading the Bible at the time?

Of the different ways of reading the Bible covered here (e.g. copying, biblical meditation, praying psalms, etc.), which have you tried already? Which would you like to try? Which do you most struggle with?

As a group, choose a short passage of Scripture (perhaps one mentioned in this chapter), and with coloured pens and paper, spend some time silently copying out the passage and illuminating with patterns or illustrations. Afterwards share any thoughts or reflections on the activity.

Pray through a psalm together, reading it aloud as a group. If you want to practise praying through psalms quickly you could use the psalms of ascent (Psalms 120–134), designed to be prayed by pilgrims to Jerusalem in preparation for worship.

Where in your life could you make room for mindful study of the Bible?

Mindful Reflection

A number of years ago I spent a glorious summer's day on a small mountain:

I'm sitting on a rock; I feel its smoothness and hardness and then the warmth of the sun on my skin. I can smell the heady scent of heather. It's almost overwhelming – so strong I can practically taste honey. I feel happy, at peace. Gazing at the beauty of the landscape, words from a well-known hymn pop into my mind: "… The purple-headed mountain, the river running by… "[1] I'm aware of a full feeling as I take in the view. I notice the ground around me and am amazed by the minute and intricate beauty of moss and lichen. Such tiny created beauty! Climbing to the summit, I feel the power of the wind buffeting my body and recognize a sense of my own smallness in the vast space around me. I feel awe. I feel I'm bursting with emotion – with thankfulness, and find myself wanting to shout out psalms of praise. Then I see a man coming. I feel concern, alone, nervous, vulnerable. We pass on the path and I feel relief. Later, I'm standing on the mountainside moved to tears at the sight of litter strewn among the heather. I feel sadness, sorrow, grief. Grief expands beyond the mountain to a broken world. Then peace, love, and gratitude…

These rich and varied experiences happened during a week taken to spend time out with God. It was part of a guided retreat in which the activities and exercises involved were individually suggested to me by a spiritual director. The day I wrote was a day primarily of being rather than of doing, of being in the present moment out on the mountain with God. It was also part of a reflective process of becoming more conscious of how various experiences, external and internal pressures, urges, or events were impacting on my choices and the way I was living out my faith.

Later, when reflecting on that day, I noticed that I had been able to be more aware than usual, attending to what was going on around and within me at a deeper level. I was aware of a sense of thankfulness and gratitude for all I had received – for the experience of being caught up in the creativity and love of God. My focus was drawn to the time I saw the man on the mountain. Staying with those uncomfortable feelings I noticed that I had projected my fears onto him. What I experienced was part of, and drew me deeper into, attending to God, in prayer. My focus moved to the time of tears. All those feelings of sadness were still vivid, and then I glimpsed a recognition of a sense of my own part in the destructiveness of humanity and somewhere in it all the compassion of God… and so went deeper into prayer.

Being on retreat created space for me to be more aware and reflective, or to put it another way, more mindful. While it is not possible to live with such a degree of focused awareness all the time, being mindful and reflective has long been an important aspect of spiritual practice within Christian tradition. Such practices are valuable in deepening our relationship with God and in encouraging increasing integration and intentionality in the way faith is expressed in our lives. In particular, they can help us to notice where and how we experience God's presence or absence in the busyness of our daily lives, what draws us towards or away from God, and what helps or hinders us in living as Jesus' disciples.

While there are many different and valuable ways of fostering such mindful spiritual practice, this chapter focuses on Ignatian spirituality, the story that lies behind it, and the key role played by awareness.

Before exploring these further, we need to travel back in time to the year 1521 ...

The tale of a would-be romantic hero

It is the month of May. Battle is raging as the French army attacks the besieged city of Pamplona. Twenty-six-year-old Iñigo Lopez de Loyola rallies the Spanish defence but in the heat of the fight he is struck in the legs by a cannonball and seriously wounded.

Disheartened by his fall, the other soldiers surrender and the city is taken. The French are so impressed by Iñigo's courage that they release him to be returned to his ancestral home. There he undergoes brutal surgery that he will later describe as "butchery", first to reset his bones and then a second time to avoid disfigurement. He becomes extremely ill and nearly dies.[2]

Move forward several months... Iñigo is making a good, if long, recovery. Unable to stand and confined to his bed, he asks for some books to read to while away the time. He's hoping for the kind of romantic fiction he enjoys but has to be content with the only books available: Spanish translations of Ludolf of Saxony's *Life of Christ* and a book of the *Lives of the Saints*.[3]

When not reading he spends time daydreaming about a certain lady he knows, of poetry he will write for her, and of gallant actions he will perform in her honour. At other times he imagines himself acting in ways similar to saints, or spiritual heroes. Over time he begins to notice subtle differences in his emotions. While daydreaming of courtly romance he senses much "delight" but afterwards feels "dry and dissatisfied". However, when imagining acts of spiritual heroism, he notices that he is "cheerful and satisfied" both during his daydreams and afterwards. He begins to "wonder at the difference and to reflect on it, learning from experience that one kind of thoughts left him sad and the other cheerful". In this he recognizes that some thoughts draw him towards God and some pull him away from God.[4]

These insights lead him to reflect on his previous life and into a process of conversion. For the rest of his life, this passionate, courageous soldier who by his own admission was previously "given over to the vanities of the world... with a great and vain desire of winning glory"[5] will devote himself wholeheartedly and single-mindedly to the service of Jesus.

Help... I'm a Geek

Further reading in this area

Background reading: Ignatius' story in his own words and a selection of his letters for those interested to find out more about the man himself:

de Cámara, L. G. (1556). *Ignatius' Own Story with a Sampling of his Letters.* (W. J. Young, tr. 1956). Chicago, IL: Loyola University Press.

A classic translation of the Spiritual Exercises. Not an easy read, this is really a handbook, or guide, written for those who give the Spiritual Exercises:

Puhl, L. J. (1952). *The Spiritual Exercises of St Ignatius: Based on Studies in the Language of the Autograph.* Chicago, IL: Loyola University Press.

For beginners, a helpful and accessible introduction to and presentation of the Spiritual Exercises:

Muldoon, T. (2004). *The Ignatian Workout: Daily Spiritual Exercises for a Healthy Faith*. Chicago, IL: Loyola Press.

For a more technical approach try:

Lonsdale, D. (1990). *Eyes to See, Ears to Hear: An Introduction to Ignatian Spirituality*. London: Darton, Longman & Todd.

Written in a conversational style by a Jesuit out of his own experiences of and reflections on undertaking the Spiritual Exercises and directing others through them. This book gives an insight into the Exercises and contains much valuable spiritual wisdom:

English, J. (2003). *Spiritual Freedom*. (2nd ed.). Chicago, IL: Loyola University Press.

For a useful Internet resource for background on Ignatian Spirituality, Ignatius of Loyola, the Spiritual Exercises, and the Daily Examen go to: www.jesuits.org/spirituality

A complete list of sources is provided in the reference section at the end of the book.

The pilgrim pupil

In recounting his story to Luis Gonzales de Camara, Iñigo, or Ignatius as he is more commonly known, speaks of himself as "the pilgrim",[6] reflecting his ongoing spiritual journey. Following his recovery and conversion, he spent a year in Manresa during which he underwent a further period of formative growth and change. Describing this time, he says, "God treated him just as a schoolmaster treats a little boy when he teaches him."[7] Despite experiencing what he describes as the most profound spiritual revelation of his life, these months in Manresa proved deeply challenging at times.[8] It is clear that he learned a great deal from various excesses, mistakes, and temptations. He would continue to draw on these experiences in his own life of faith, in his thinking about spiritual discernment, and in his subsequent writing.

Learning from our experience

Learning from subjective experience is a natural process involved in human development. It is something we do from our earliest days and for the rest of our lives. So perhaps it is not surprising that Ignatius' learning, both during his recovery and then in Manresa, should be primarily experiential. It was rooted in the events of his daily life and in observation of his shifting emotional responses and desires. In reflecting on these experiences he began to recognize God's presence and the work of the Holy Spirit in his life; the perceptions and understanding gained from these reflections became the basis for his subsequent decisions and actions.[9] This process is not that dissimilar to some modern psychological thinking about how we learn and develop.

The psychologist David Kolb defines learning as "the process whereby knowledge is created through the transformation of experience".[10] He suggests this is a complex and interactive process that involves:

- undergoing concrete experience

- reflecting on that experience

- integration of these reflections into more abstract ideas

- putting the ideas into practice, which opens up further learning experiences.[11]

**Concrete
Experience**
*(doing / having an
experience)*

**Active
Experimentation**
*(planning / trying out
what you have learned)*

**Reflective
Observation**
*(reviewing / reflecting on
the experience)*

**Abstract
Conceptualization**
*(concluding / learning
from the experience)*

Get Some Exercise!

One or more practical exercises

For more examples of and information on the Examen of Consciousness and Ignatian reflective prayer the following websites are helpful:

www.jesuits.org/spirituality

www.ignatianspirituality.com/ignatian-prayer/the-examen

www.beunos.com/prayerexamen.htm

Although at first sight this may look like a children's book it is for adults. It offers a variety of approaches to the Examen and suggestions for its use with individuals, families, and groups:

Linn, D., Linn, S. F. & Linn, M. (1995). *Sleeping with Bread: Holding What Gives You Life.* Mahwah, NJ: Paulist Press.

Another useful book of spiritual exercises written by a Jesuit priest and spiritual guide that draws on both Scripture and Eastern and Western spiritual traditions is:

De Mello, A. (1978). *Sadhana: A Way to God – Christian Exercises in Eastern Form.* New York: Bantam Doubleday Dell Publishing Group.

Many of these exercises are similar to mindfulness exercises.

Kolb sees this process as being closely related to and leading to development.[12] Quoting the American philosopher, John Dewey, he describes "each episode of experience [as filled] with the potential for movement from blind impulse to a life of choice and purpose".[13] However, he stresses that experience on its own does not necessarily lead to much learning. In order to learn from experience we need consciously and intentionally to engage with the whole process of reflection, abstract thinking, and practical action.[14]

Ignatius is often described as an early psychologist, because he seems to have done precisely this. Drawing on episodes in his own learning experience, he developed existing spiritual practices in a way that encouraged others to notice and reflect on their experience as a way of finding deeper freedom in their choices and subsequent actions.

Exercises leading to freedom and fitness

From his own account, it is evident that Ignatius felt a strong call to enable others in their discipleship and within five years of his conversion he had distilled his experiential learning into a series of Spiritual Exercises that he gave to those seeking his help.[15] He describes these Spiritual Exercises as consisting of "every method of examination of conscience, of meditation, of contemplation, of vocal and mental prayer, and of other spiritual activities".[16] He sees them as exercises for the soul, a means of getting spiritually fit, likening them to physical exercises for bodily well-being. This idea of exercising for "spiritual fitness" has been taken up in recent times by Bishop Graham Tomlin in his book of the same name.[17] The aim of the exercises is to enable the person undertaking them to find freedom from things that hinder and block the Holy Spirit's work in his or her life and freedom to respond more wholeheartedly in service to God.[18]

Yes... but...

Isn't this introspective and disconnected from the real world?

There is probably always a risk of this in any practice where we turn our attention to inner lives. However, Ignatian spiritual exercises are grounded in the reality of our daily lives and recognize the presence of God who engages with us in that reality; in turn they encourage us to engage with those around us and the real world.

Ignatius' understanding of the interior movements of consolation and desolation that we experience allows us to discern the direction that we are moving in at different times. Practice of the Examen of Consciousness helps us to be aware of and mindful of our day-to-day living and interactions with those around us. It helps us to be open to the transformative action of the Holy Spirit in our lives and to become more Christ-like. This will in turn lead us into deeper engagement, compassion, and love for those around us.

The Ignatian Spiritual Exercises are given during time set aside specifically for this purpose, either during a thirty-day retreat or over a number of months during the course of everyday life. While Ignatius suggests the use of a number of methods of prayer in the Spiritual Exercises, perhaps the one most well-known and distinctive is known as "imaginative contemplation". This is a way of prayerfully engaging with Bible narratives in regular hour-long prayer sessions that form part of the retreat. This requires the individual to make use of his imagination and senses (sight, sound, smell, taste, and touch) in order to be fully present to the passage he is contemplating, as if he were there witnessing the biblical events in person. This is not an end in itself but rather a way of enabling him to get in touch with his responses to the passage and also with his deepest desires. He is asked to notice what is going on within himself in a non-judgmental way, to be mindful of his inner experience. He then takes what he observes into honest and open conversation with God.

Where are we headed?

Following the prayer hour the individual is asked to take ten to fifteen minutes to reflect prayerfully on any inner urges, states, or movements that he has noticed. In this Ignatius is concerned with enabling people to grow in discernment, in interpreting these inner movements, in sensitivity to the Holy Spirit's work within them, and in making the best choices. Drawing on his own experience he recognizes that we experience the pull of different forces in our lives. He distinguishes between two contrary interior movements that he calls "consolation" and "desolation". Consolation is any felt movement, state, or desire that draws us closer to God and outwards towards others while desolation draws us away from God and others and into self-absorption. Discernment is essential in understanding these movements as it is not always obvious which is which; both can be experienced positively or negatively and even the experience of desolation can be helpful in our growth. The key factor is the ultimate direction of the movements observed.[19] This discernment can be helped greatly by a trusted, wise Christian friend or mentor.[20]

Daily mindful spiritual practice

Ignatius regarded discernment as a vital part of spiritual growth and development, important not only in times of retreat but also as a regular aspect of day-to-day Christian discipleship. This was because he recognized that it is in the midst of the messiness of our human existence that we encounter God and grow in him. He therefore encouraged the practice of another awareness exercise, the "Examen of Consciousness", in daily life.[21]

This involves attending without judgment to the experiences and events within our daily lives and to the thoughts, feelings, attitudes, longings, and desires we notice arising within us as we do this.[22] This mindful and reflective practice is primarily concerned with awareness that leads to discernment. Attentive awareness allows us to be in touch with who we really are, our true self, and with the false self that we may present to others. It also enables us to observe the things that we may allow to control our lives or that we are overly or inappropriately attached to, things that may be hindering our response to and growth in God.[23] In terms of mindful discipleship this practice enables that ongoing process that Paul speaks of: "Do not conform [any longer] to the pattern of this world, but be transformed by the renewing of your mind. Then you will be able to test and approve what God's will is – his good, pleasing and perfect will" (Romans 12:2) and "this is my prayer: that your love may abound more and more in knowledge and depth of insight, so that you may be able to discern what is best and may be pure and blameless for the day of Christ" (Philippians 1:9–10).

While the Examen of Consciousness traditionally involved five stages, it is highly adaptable. It can be as simple as asking, "What am I most grateful for today and what am I least grateful for?", "Where have I been conscious of God's presence today and where have I experienced his absence?", or even "What was your best part of the day and what was the worst part?"[24] It can be performed at any time of the day, at different intervals and at different levels. It can be done alone or with others and it is accessible to all ages.

Although some people reverse the first and second steps, generally the Examen of Consciousness follows this structure:

- Become aware of God's presence.

- Review the day with gratitude.

- Pay attention to your emotions.

- Choose one feature of the day and pray from it.

- Look toward tomorrow.[25]

Here is a more fully worked example:

- Come to God, Father, Son, and Holy Spirit, in a spirit of gratitude and allow yourself to be relaxed, secure in the knowledge of his love, expressing thankfulness for all his good gifts to you.

- Ask for the Holy Spirit's light, guidance, and help to be aware of those things God would have you notice during the time period (e.g. previous twenty-four hours or week) that you are attending to.

- Without forcing your focus on anything, allow your attention to rest on those events that come to the forefront of your mind, and without judging notice what you feel as you sit with them. See if there is one particular area you are drawn to. Notice where you have been aware or not aware of God's presence, where you have been drawn towards God or away from him.

- Talk with Jesus as with a friend about the things you have noticed and the responses that they raise within you. Express thanks or sorrow, or ask for forgiveness as appropriate.

- Ask God for the help that you need during the coming day or period of time. You may like to end this time by saying the Lord's Prayer.

Something that stands out in this practice is that it is undertaken in a spirit of *gratitude*. Although it has not been mentioned very much so far, gratitude pervades the Spiritual Exercises. The practice of gratitude is explored in a later chapter but it is worth noting its importance within the Examen of Consciousness. Approaching God with thanksgiving takes our focus away from ourselves and allows us to recognize the unmerited generosity – the grace – of God, not only in all that is given to us, but also the ways in which we are held and sustained in his love. It makes us aware of our dependence on his compassion and kindness, and enables us to see ourselves in a different way. Being reminded of signs of God's love for us enables us to be open to what the Holy Spirit will reveal during the process and naturally leads us to ask for the help we need to notice this. As we engage with Jesus in reflecting on what we have noticed during the Examen we are again moved to give thanks. It is from the place of gratitude and trust that we ask in faith for the help we need in going forward.

A recent talk by Jon Kabat-Zinn shows some parallels between mindfulness as practised in a therapeutic context and the Ignatian disciplines of Examen of Consciousness and reflective prayer. He speaks of mindfulness as "a way of connecting with your life" and of it giving us "new degrees of freedom to navigate life" as it allows us not to be "at the mercy of our own thoughts and drive".[26] However, despite these parallels, the direction of travel is different. For the follower of Jesus, engaging in mindful spiritual practices such as the Ignatian exercises is about connecting us ever more deeply with the one who is our Life – Jesus. It is about discerning where we are headed, but above all a way of turning to God (repenting). It's about cooperating with the Spirit's desire to free us from all that blocks and hinders our life in God, so that we are free to serve the one who loves us beyond measure and gives himself for us, Jesus. After all, the community that Ignatius founded is called the "Society of *Jesus*".

When Two or Three are Gathered...

Questions for group discussion

You may like to use the following questions to discuss mindful reflection as a small group.

Has anyone in the group attended an organized retreat or taken a retreat day for themselves? Tell the group about what you did and what it was like.

Ignatius emphasized learning by reflecting on our experience. What experiences have you had lately that have caused you to reflect and perhaps grow spiritually?

Think about moments of consolation (drawing us closer to God and others) and desolation (cutting us off from God and others). Over the last twenty-four hours, what have been your moments of consolation and desolation?

What help or assistance do you think you will need from God in the coming twenty-four hours? Pray this together.

Character

Mindfulness and Christian Character

Real Christianity

William Wilberforce (1759–1833) is best known as a moral and political reformer. His most famous accomplishment is no doubt the central role he played in championing the Slavery Abolition Act, which ended the slave trade across the majority of the British empire. It was passed in 1833, shortly before his death. He was buried in Westminster Abbey close to his friend and political ally, William Pitt. His epitaph reads, "In a country fertile in great and good men, he was among the foremost of those who fixed the character of their time".

Where Did it Come From?

The game with minutes

For generations, Christians have proposed that we can learn to be like Christ by making time to be mindful of his presence.

Perhaps most famously Nicolas Herman (1614–1691), otherwise known as Brother Lawrence, a lay brother in the Carmelite order, outlined a series of exercises for practising awareness of God's presence during his kitchen duties in the monastery. He called it practising the presence of God.

In more recent years, Frank Laubach (1884–1970), the educator and missionary, advocated what he called the "game with minutes". He recommended that all Christians experiment with keeping God in mind for at least one second of every minute of every day. This constant mystical connection with God was the powerhouse behind his monumental international efforts for world peace, justice, and literacy.

Both Brother Lawrence and Frank Laubach extolled the practice of keeping God in mind as a way of developing Christ-like character.

It was a fitting tribute, because beyond political reform, Wilberforce had sought not just to change the power structures of his era, but to transform the entire moral character of his nation. With this aim in view, in 1797, he published a short volume with the catchy title: *A Practical View of the Prevailing Religious System of Professed Christians in the Higher and Middle Classes of This Country Contrasted with Real Christianity*. Those were indeed the days of very long book titles. It is difficult to imagine a book with a title that verbose flying off the shelves of modern booksellers, but by the standards of its day it was a bestseller. It sold 7,500 copies within six months and was translated into numerous languages. We know it today by its abbreviated title: *Real Christianity*.

When asked to state the purpose of his book, Wilberforce responded that his aim was to "make goodness fashionable". He wished to elevate the moral climate of his age and he aimed to do so by addressing himself to the moral lives of his contemporaries. He endeavoured to bring about a change in their character. This was the Real Christianity he had in mind.

Mindfulness and morality

Mindfulness has always been linked to moral qualities of character. The historical traditions that have taught mindful practices have done so with the aim of improving the character of those who adopt them. Whether it was the Buddhists seeking to develop lovingkindness or the desert fathers seeking holiness through meditative practice, mindfulness was intended to be a formational activity. Being mindful was viewed as a pathway to being moral.

Mindfulness and morality go together like peas and carrots, but in contemporary Western society the link tends to be de-emphasized. Being mindful is more often promoted as a route to psychological health than as a means of moral improvement. It can be viewed as a technique for addressing the problems that plague our culture, such as stress, depression, or low self-esteem. Or alternatively, celebrated as a way of developing positive qualities such as creativity, compassion, acceptance, or the ability to focus. The link between mindfulness and "the good life" continues to be stressed, but the good life is now largely couched in psychological rather than ethical terms.

Yes... but...

Is it right to learn from non-Christian sources?

Some Christians have expressed concern over projects like the VIA handbook of character strengths and virtues, that draw insight from numerous other religions and ideologies.

The fear behind this objection is that we may contaminate or devalue our commitment to the Lord Jesus Christ by looking elsewhere for guidance on how to live.

However, it is worth remembering that there is a long history of biblical writers drawing wisdom from sources beyond the Judeo-Christian faith. Many of the proverbs assembled by Solomon and his contemporaries were directly drawn from other Middle Eastern or Egyptian sources, selected and edited to become advice on godly living. The apostle Paul also was prepared to cite pagan sources, such as Epimenides and Aratus, in communicating the gospel (Acts 17:28). Even many contemporary Bible teachers use the language and media of our time to communicate truth more clearly.

Truth is truth wherever we find it. We shouldn't be surprised that people all over the world reflecting deeply on the best way to live have at times come to similar conclusions. We can be open to these without jeopardizing our commitment to the core tenets of the Christian faith.

The psychology of character

Throughout much of the twentieth century, psychologists have been reluctant to make use of the word "character". It has been viewed as too vague to belong to a scientific discipline that prizes only that which is observable and measurable. Character fell out of fashion in mainstream psychology and, apart from the occasional innovator or rogue academic, the concept fell into disuse.

By the turn of the millennium, however, things had begun to change. There were various signs that psychologists were warming again to the notion of character, to see it once more as a useful concept for the discipline. The most public expression of this arrived in 2004 with the publication of *Character Strengths and Virtues: A Handbook and Classification*.[1] It was a landmark volume arriving at the conclusion of a three-year multimillion-dollar project. It was funded by the VIA Institute for Character, based in Cincinnati,[2] and involved more than fifty leading scientists and scholars.

The first phase of the project aimed to identify what has been viewed as good character across the planet throughout recorded history. With this in mind it gathered several hundred historical documents stretching back 2,500 years, drawing on the traditions of Athenian philosophy, Buddhism, Hinduism, Taoism, Islam, Judaism, and Christianity. The sources were wide-ranging, from

Aristotle's *Nicomachean Ethics* to the knightly virtues of King Charlemagne, from the pithy diatribes of Lord Baden-Powell to the Sermon on the Mount.

Painstaking analysis of all these documents resulted in the identification of six core virtues reputed to be celebrated by all people at all times: wisdom and knowledge, courage, humanity, justice, temperance, and transcendence. Attached to these was a list of twenty-four character strengths that can be defined, spotted, measured, and developed. The list was as follows:

1. Knowledge: creativity, curiosity, perspective, love of learning, judgment

2. Courage: bravery, honesty, zest, perseverance

3. Humanity: kindness, love, social intelligence

4. Justice: teamwork, fairness, leadership

5. Temperance: humility, prudence, self-regulation, forgiveness

6. Transcendence: hope, humour, spirituality, gratitude, appreciation of beauty.[3]

Since the publication of this catalogue of strengths and virtues literally thousands of research projects have been conducted looking at them.[4] Over a million people worldwide have completed the strengths survey associated with the scheme, and in the last decade it has been validated in seventy-five different nations.[5] Character as a useful concept for psychologists is back with a vengeance. Character strength from this point of view is who we are when we are at our best.

The happiness donut

Many scholars have been critical of the list of psychological strengths and virtues that the VIA team came up with. Some have called it "the happiness donut",[6] implying that such virtuous qualities are all well and good, but that standing alone like this, they lack any sense of coherence or central focus. Some Christians would argue that this unifying centre can be found by locating these qualities in Jesus. Other scholars have complained that, in the development of Christ-like character, it is inappropriate to look to other faith traditions such as Buddhism, Islam, or even Greek philosophy for insight, when this may draw us away from exclusive devotion to Christ.

By the Book

Being with Jesus and becoming like Jesus

In the Gospel of John, Jesus explicitly links bearing fruit with the practice of resting in him. He says, "I am the vine, you are the branches. Whoever abides in me and I in him, he it is that bears much fruit" (John 15:5 ESV).

The word often translated "abide" (menō) in this passage has incredible resonance throughout the New Testament. It occurs 127 times in 105 verses, and most of the time it is translated, "to stay or to remain". When Jesus looks up into a tree and informs Zacchaeus that he is coming to stay at his house, it is the word menō that is used (Luke 19:5). When the disciples on the Emmaus Road beg the resurrected Christ, whom they fail to recognize, to stay with them for the evening, it is menō again. And when, in the Garden of Gethsemane, Jesus implores his friends to remain present and not drift off to sleep, this is the word he uses: "My soul is very sorrowful, even to death; remain [menō] here and watch with me" (Matthew 26:38 ESV).

In John's writing however it takes on special significance. It is contained in the first question Jesus is asked ("Rabbi, where are you staying?" –

John 1:38) and occurs more intensely in the first eleven verses of John 15 than anywhere else in the Bible. John uses menō twenty-four times in his first letter, and consistently links it with the development of good character: "whoever says he abides in him ought to walk in the same way in which he walked" (1 John 2:6 ESV). John was at pains to stress that it was in making space and time to accommodate Jesus in every aspect of our lives that we develop godly character. We become like Jesus, by being with him.

It is however easy to forget that Christians at other times and for other purposes have developed lists of positive qualities that look very similar to the VIA's. For example, C. S. Lewis in the appendix of his short book *The Abolition of Man*[7] offers a series of worldwide examples of what he doesn't hesitate to call the Tao – the universal way of living manifested across cultures. One principle to which he draws attention is the fact that courage in battle appears to be a universally celebrated quality of character. In this sense the VIA classification of character strengths could be viewed as a psychological version of what apologists have called "the moral argument", the assertion that the presence of a sense of right and wrong in all people, wherever and whenever we find them, is a signpost to the existence of a moral creator.

The New Testament of course contains numerous passages that could be considered lists of virtues or the fruit of godly living. Take Paul's list of the fruit of the Spirit in Galatians 5 for example. He suggests that those who live in accordance with the Holy Spirit will bear the fruit of godly character with qualities such as love, joy, peace, patience, kindness, goodness, faithfulness, gentleness, and self-control coming to the fore (Galatians 5:22–23). Or take Peter's catalogue of what he calls "supplements" to our faith: virtue, knowledge, self-control, steadfastness, godliness, brotherly affection, and love (2 Peter 1:5–7). All of which, according to him, are to be pursued and developed by those who wish to be effective in the Christian life. Jesus himself begins the Sermon on the Mount in Matthew's Gospel commending eight qualities of character. He blesses, among others, the poor in spirit, the humble, the merciful, and the pure-hearted as those to whom the kingdom of heaven is especially applicable (Matthew 5:3–10).

Help... I'm a Geek

Further reading in character strengths

For a thorough theological grounding in the rationale for character development from a leading New Testament scholar you could look at:

Wright, N. T. (2010). *Virtue Reborn*. London: SPCK.

Similarly, an extensive treatment of the integration of theological and psychological approaches to character formation can be found in:

Collicutt, J. (2015). *The Psychology of Christian Character Formation*. London: SCM Press.

A complete outline of Ryan Niemiec's approach, Mindfulness Based Strengths Practice (MBSP), is offered in:

Niemiec, R. M. (2014). *Mindfulness and Character Strengths: A Practical Guide to Flourishing*. Boston, MA: Hogrefe.

An early summary of the VIA classification of strengths can be obtained in this article:

Park, N., Peterson, C. & Seligman, M. E. P. (2004). Strengths of character and well-being. *Journal of Social and Clinical Psychology*, 23(5), pages 603–619.

A full list of sources is provided in the reference section at the end of the book.

There are numerous lists of beautiful qualities of character in the Bible that deserve our attention. The problem is that we tend not to dwell on them too much. We can easily skip over them quickly in our daily Bible reading. We give them a cursory glance, but can fail to look deeply into them. Paul the apostle tells us not to do that. He writes that we should let our minds focus upon good things; that we should ruminate and rest our attention on that which is excellent; to think about that which is true, noble, right, pure, lovely, and honourable (Philippians 4:8). This is where a mindful attitude can help us.

Mindful strengths use

In recent years, Ryan Niemiec, Education Director of the VIA Institute for Character, has developed an elegant and systematic approach to the integration of mindfulness with character strengths. He developed an eight-session programme entitled Mindfulness Based Strengths Practice (MBSP),[8] which combines the development of psychological strengths and virtues with the practice of mindfulness. From his perspective mindfulness and character development can be combined in two major ways. We can practise "mindful strengths use" by bringing focused attention to strengths of character, such as humility, gratitude, love, or wisdom, thereby nurturing and expanding our use of them. On the other hand we can adopt "strong mindfulness" whereby we bring character strengths such as self-control, curiosity, or compassion to our practice of mindfulness to assist us in being non-judgmentally aware of ourselves and the world around us.[9]

Get Some Exercise!

Being mindful of character strengths

This exercise is adapted from "mindful strengths use" in Ryan Niemiec's book, *Mindfulness and Character Strengths*. It is designed to help us spot positive qualities of character in ourselves and in others and thereby develop them. It can be outlined in a series of simple steps.

Learn the language of good character. If we wish to value and dwell upon the good things that God is developing in us, we need to be attentive to this and be able to recognize it. For this purpose we may wish to learn the VIA strengths list off by heart. Or alternatively, take biblical lists of virtue (e.g. Matthew 5:3–10; Galatians 5:22–23; Philippians 4:8; 2 Peter 1:5–7) and commit them to memory. At least then we know what we are looking for.

Learn to look and listen for strengths. You can spot these in yourself and in others. They can be noticed in times when we "light up", become more alert, our energy rises, speech becomes more assertive, and hope or joy are in evidence. We need to practise spotting good in other people like this over and over again to become good at it.

Label character strengths when you see them. Both in yourself and in others, give a label that associates an observed behaviour with a character strength. For example, when you notice someone being willing to allow others to share the praise for a team accomplishment, label it as humility. Or if you see someone who presses on with a project in spite of stress and opposition, you can label it persistence.

Express appreciation. Having spotted and labelled a strength, you may wish to express appreciation for it. Sometimes this will be directly to someone else: "I'm really appreciative of the kindness you continue to show me." Or it may be that you thank God privately for a person's kindness or hope or so on. With regard to yourself, you can thank God that he has given you the courage, for example, to confront a difficult colleague or family member.

Pray positively. You can also be mindful of character strengths by spotting places where they are lacking but needed. You can pray for hope for people who are suffering under depression or discouragement. Or ask God for wisdom when facing a difficult decision.

The first of these, "mindful strengths use", may be of particular interest to Christians, because it invites us to focus upon areas of our lives where the development of godly character may have been neglected or may be calling for our attention. The adjacent text box offers detailed instructions on how to go about this.

Negativity bias

Perhaps the principal reason that mindful strengths use can be so beneficial to Christians seeking to live a godly life is that it counteracts the habitual negativity bias that bedevils the human race. The human brain, it would appear, is designed to identify and solve problems. In other words, you and I have an inherent tendency to pay attention to the bad and ignore the good. Just think for a moment of any time you've received feedback on something you've done. Maybe it was a driving instructor debriefing your parallel parking, or a teacher giving feedback on an essay, or your boss meeting with you about a project. In all these situations we tend to give more weight to the negative comments we receive and almost entirely delete the positive.[10]

A few weeks ago, a friend of mine was telling me about offering training to a church and flicking through the feedback forms afterwards. The complimentary comments were overwhelming. He had done a great job and the congregation were all deeply appreciative. All, that is, apart from one form. The feedback on this form was equally complimentary but then, as a point for improvement, suggested that my friend could be "more enthusiastic" in his presentation. Instantly, the warm glow of having done a good job was stripped away, and replaced by the concern that his presentational style lacked the required passion. Somehow the single negative comment outweighed all the positives. The compliments felt nice, but the criticism felt true.

This is the negativity bias in action. Presenting to a crowd of 100 smiling faces, we will be drawn to the one that looks bored. After a day of many blessings, it is the frustrations and annoyances that linger in our minds that evening. Switch on the nightly news and mostly it will be bad news. Even in everyday conversation it is the scandalous gossip that we find most delicious. We are primed to look out for and think upon negative information.

There is of course good reason for this. More often than not it is negative information that requires immediate action from us. It is therefore functional to scan our environments for signs of danger, or threat, and be ready to respond quickly when they are detected. The problem is that our negativity detection system is hyperactive – stuck on overdrive – it would have us obsessing exclusively on the negative while completely ignoring the positive. This can be particularly problematic when it comes to the development of good character.

Commending the good

We can gauge the extent to which we have trained our minds to focus upon the good, by how skilled we are in speaking about good things in other people. In the workplace, school, or church our language for giving negative feedback to people can often be so much more sophisticated than our ability to elaborate on the good in them. We tend to be so much more adept at criticism than we are at compliment.

One psychologist likened the feedback we offer to other people to the suits in a deck of playing cards. We can tell people what we think of them in four different ways.[11] *Clubs* feedback involves telling people that they did things wrong without any further detail. It can be a sharp rebuke. It guarantees they won't do it again, but goes no further. *Spades* feedback on the other hand indicates where they got it wrong and digs deep into the detail of precisely what they got wrong and how. Conversely, *hearts* feedback is positive, it tells someone they are fantastic, but not much more. It may leave them wondering why we think that about them and whether we are really sincere. It can be difficult to tell the difference between a vague compliment and an insincere platitude.

All three of these styles of feedback to other people – clubs, spades, and hearts – have their place, but the research suggests that if we really wish to bring the best out in other people we will learn to give *diamonds* feedback. This means that we attend to the good in them in great detail. We apply Paul's advice to our relationships, we look for the good, the true, the noble, the pure, and we make the most of it wherever we find it. We become every bit as skilful in commending the good as we are in complaining about the bad.

By applying the same principle to ourselves, therefore, mindful strengths use can help us in our own spiritual formation. It suggests that we take a moment to focus on the good things developing in us, to be aware of them, expand them, and practise them. By intentionally directing our attention and energy towards the seeds of love, hope, faith, gentleness, truthfulness, or discretion that are germinating within us we can gain insight into how best to cooperate with the Holy Spirit in bringing them to fruition. We work with God in the formation of our character for the good of others.

Mini-rests and micro-sabbaths

There is another way that being mindful can help us in the development of Christian character. The word often applied to positive qualities of character in the Bible is the word "fruit" (or *karpos* in New Testament Greek), and the most intensive occurrence of this word can be found in the opening verses of chapter fifteen of John's Gospel. *Karpos*, the same word for fruit used by Paul to denote the evidence of a spirit-filled life, is used by Jesus seven times in eleven verses (John 15:1–11). In the same passage it is closely associated with another Greek word, *menō* (often translated to abide, to stay, or to remain). Jesus links bearing fruit with abiding: "whoever abides in me and I in him, he it is that bears much fruit" (John 15:5 ESV).

In John 15, Jesus seems to be suggesting that bearing the fruit of good character hinges not just on concentrating our minds on the good, but on learning to remain in his presence, that fixing our thoughts and intentions on him is the way to develop Christ-like character. And this is where a mindful attitude to Christ in prayer can be so very helpful. Not rushing through a shopping list of requests or rapidly scanning a few pages of Scripture, but pressing the pause button and taking a moment to be with Jesus.

While our lives may be time-poor they are moment-rich. Day by day, hour by hour, life offers us numerous moments to pause and rest with God, if only we are prepared to take them. Unfortunately most of the time we don't recognize them. We call them hassles or frustrations. The queue at the supermarket checkout, the traffic jam on the way to work, the overly talkative colleague, or the slow-functioning laptop. But if, instead of spinning the wheels of our mind in frustration, we can be mindfully in the moment, all of these can become mini-rests, or micro-sabbaths, in which we meet with Jesus.

Nourishing character

The counsellor Brian Thorne[12] tells the story of a simple Norfolk farmer who fell into the habit of spending hours each day alone in his local village chapel. So much so that his vicar became concerned for him and eventually decided to enquire as to what exactly he was up to. The farmer said that he was spending his time praying. When pressed further on what exactly he had to pray about that filled so many hours, he innocently responded, "Not much, I just looks at 'im and 'ee just looks at me." He was taking a moment to be mindful of God. And this abiding, according to Jesus, is the nursery in which the seedlings of godly character are nourished.

When Two or Three are Gathered...

Questions for small group discussion

You may like to use the following questions to discuss character development as a small group.

Do a bit of strengths-spotting for a moment. When you look at the other members of the group, what good qualities of character do you see in them? In what way do they present the character of God to you? Tell them.

Read aloud the different lists of virtues discussed in this chapter (VIA; Matthew 5:3–10; Galatians 5:22–23; Philippians 4:8; 2 Peter 1:5–7). What differences do you notice between the biblical lists and the VIA strengths?

Of the qualities of good character mentioned, which do you feel in most need of at present? Where and how would it help you if you developed more of this quality?

The chapter suggests that we can develop more Christ-like character by taking more time to be mindful of Christ. How do you currently make time for Jesus in your life? Do you have any ideas about how you could make more space for him?

If you were to commit to the development of good character over the next few weeks, what if anything would you continue to do? What, if anything, would you do differently?

Mindful Gratitude

Where good happens suddenly

Not many people know that when J. R. R. Tolkien first wrote *The Lord of the Rings*, back in the days before it was a Hollywood blockbuster complete with special effects, he had a particular principle in mind. Behind his tale of elves and orcs, hobbits and dwarves was a simple idea.

He noted that we all know what a catastrophe is. One of those terrible moments in history where the smallest thing – a nuclear bomb the size of a cricket ball, the tiniest shift in an undersea tectonic plate, the hijacking of a passenger jet – becomes the catalyst that unleashes terror and devastation affecting thousands of lives. We are familiar with these occurrences, we see them on the nightly news. But what we are less familiar with, claimed Tolkien, are those occasions when the opposite happens. Those moments when, against all the odds, the smallest act of bravery or kindness, love or forgiveness, releases something beautiful into the world and momentarily stems the tide of destruction and evil.

Where Did it Come From?

A historical example of gratitude practice

Since the time of Jesus, Christians have recommended gratitude practices similar to those explored in modern psychology. A wide variety of exercises have been developed to help people express their thankfulness to God.

One example comes from Francis de Sales (1567–1622), Bishop of Geneva, in his *Introduction to the Devout Life*. In his third meditation he recommends that, in prayerfulness, the believer should reflect upon the extent of the gifts that God has given. He advises that we kindle our gratitude, by taking a moment to dwell on the ways in which material needs have been met, friendships formed, and hardships overcome during the course of our lives. And furthermore, we remind ourselves of the love and forgiveness God has shown us in Jesus. All of these are gifts from God, and Francis taught his disciples to give thanks every morning and evening, as part of their spiritual formation.

This was the idea that lay behind his trilogy, the epic narrative of a hobbit, the humblest of creatures, ending an empire of evil with a single courageous, costly act. Events like this, Tolkien said, needed a new word to describe them. The word catastrophe, derived from the Greek *kata-* meaning "down" and *-strophe* meaning "turning", denotes a sudden turn of events in a devastating direction, a grave misfortune. The new word Tolkien invented to describe the opposite borrowed the Greek prefix *eu-* meaning "good" or "faring well". He christened those incredible moments in history when things take an unexpected and dramatic turn for the better, *eucatastrophes*. The story of Frodo is a story of eucatastrophe, a story where good happens suddenly.

The Greek of the New Testament is filled with words that start with Tolkien's favourite prefix. Perhaps the most famous of these is the word pronounced *euangelion*, and often translated "gospel" or "good news". At the heart of the Christian message is the ultimate eucatastrophe, the moment in which God in Jesus suffers and dies to reconcile the world to himself. Good news indeed.

But there are other significant words in the New Testament that share the same opening letters. Perhaps chief among them are the cluster of terms used to denote thankfulness or gratitude. One particular Greek word for giving thanks occurs in some of the most significant moments of the gospel narratives, and in modified form has been used by Christians globally ever since. We are of course referring to the word *eucharisteo,* from which various Christian traditions derive the word Eucharist to denote the sharing of bread and wine in communion or the Lord's Supper. When Jesus "gives thanks" for the loaves and the fishes before distributing them to a crowd of 5,000, *eucharisteō* is the verb used to indicate this. And in all four Gospels, during the Last Supper, the same word describes his thankfulness in handing his body and his blood to his disciples.

Understanding gratitude is therefore indispensable to our understanding the life of Christ as presented in the Gospels. Cultivating the practice of gratitude allows us to understand him better. Learning to be thankful ourselves is in many respects learning to be like Jesus.

The good things in life are gifts

The first time I came across formalized gratitude practice in a psychological setting was when I was delivering dialectical behaviour therapy (DBT) to adult service users in the National Health Service. DBT as an approach is specifically designed for people who self-harm or obsess about suicide. It emphasizes various forms of mindfulness as a way of managing distress and avoiding impulsive behaviour.[1]

One particular woman on the programme was quite taken with a gratefulness exercise that we had learned together, and volunteered to lead her ten-person therapy group through the exercise. She told us to sit in our chairs with our feet planted flat on the ground, and step-by-step offer silent gratitude firstly to our feet for transporting us, and then to the chair for holding our weight, and then to the floor for its firmness. In ever-widening circles, we offered silent gratitude for the calming sound of the rustling leaves at the window, for the roof that sheltered us from the rain, for the earth that held us, and for the sun that warmed us. We allowed our gratitude to stretch as far as we could in the few minutes that we had, and then returned our awareness back to the therapy room. When I opened my eyes at the end of the exercise, I was surprised to see that the woman who led us was smiling peacefully. It was lovely to see. She rarely had much to smile about.

Over the months, as she practised this gratitude exercise regularly, I began to notice many more subtle changes in her attitude. Her sense of grievance with life diminished somewhat. She had been enormously angry about the way life had treated her, and frequently bemoaned the failure of friends and staff to meet her needs adequately. But the more she practised this exercise, the happier with life she seemed to become. She learned to express her appreciation to the other members of the group and was even able to let minor insults or conflicts pass without escalating them. She became much more skilled in negotiating with other people and in making direct requests for her needs to be met. It would be misleading to suggest that she was entirely healed – emotional distress and suicidal thoughts still taunted her at times – but thankfulness had allowed her to find some comfort in her despair. Gratitude, it seemed, was the key that unlocked some freedom in her life.

It was remarkable and encouraging to watch the effect that learning gratitude had on this person's life. The improvement in her emotional well-being was undeniable. But there was something about the gratitude exercise we practised that I found quite confusing. It seemed to involve thanking inanimate objects. How, for example, could one be grateful to a chair? It seemed rather odd to beam gratefulness at the roof of a building, as if the roof would be bothered. Something about the exercise didn't make sense, it didn't sit quite right with me.

Yes... but...

Isn't thanking God entirely different from just "being grateful"?

In many ways offering prayers of thanksgiving to a loving God is a very different activity to simply generating a personal sense of gratitude for things in general.

Many of the early gratitude journaling studies were found to be just as effective when journaling was replaced by prayers of thanksgiving. And other psychological research already suggests that thanking God may be even more beneficial for well-being and personal improvement than a general sense of gratitude is. In fact, prayer itself appears to increase our levels of gratitude.

Perhaps one of the things that distinguishes thankfulness towards God from general gratitude is motive. As Christians we don't express thanks to God just because it feels good, but because it is the most appropriate response to a God who is good and has demonstrated his love in Jesus.

Only later did I begin to realize what my disquiet was about. It was actually a problem of linguistics. It is true that we tend to use the words gratitude and thankfulness interchangeably when talking about them as attitudes, but when practising them we tend to use them differently. The Benedictine monk David

Steindl-Rast[2] points out quite accurately that on the whole in everyday language, we tend to be thankful to someone, and grateful for something. We are grateful for a gift and thankful to a giver.

This subtle distinction gets us right to the heart of the psychology of gratitude. According to one of the most prominent researchers in the field, Bob Emmons, being grateful requires a pincer movement of two ways of thinking. Firstly we recognize something good in our lives. Secondly we acknowledge that the sources of this goodness originate at least partly outside of ourselves. This is gratitude in a nutshell, and explains why, according to Emmons, the journals of people who express gratitude are littered with themes of goodness, gifting, grace, and blessing. Gratitude views the good things in life as gifts.[3]

Perhaps it isn't so unusual then to be grateful for the support of a chair, the shelter of a roof, or the shade of a tree. All of them could be considered gifts to us, and therefore good reasons to be grateful.

The surprising science of gratefulness

The science of gratitude has come on in leaps and bounds over the last twenty years or so. Discovering the wide-ranging benefits of a grateful attitude has been one of the success stories of positive psychology, the worldwide movement that concerns itself with what makes human life good, moral, and meaningful.

It didn't start off quite so well though. In the early days, Bob Emmons was rather disappointed in a roomful of scholars to be assigned the task of investigating gratitude. He was hoping to be asked to study humility. And it must have been even more discouraging when Martin Seligman, the founding father of the positive psychology movement, confided in him that he just "didn't do gratitude"; hardly the most promising start to a field of research.

But within a few short years, the evidence was piling up that being grateful not only felt good, but also did people good.

Help... I'm a Geek

Further reading in gratitude studies

For a short introduction to the science of gratitude, plus a tried and tested set of exercises to follow, you may like to try:

Emmons, R. A. (2013). *Gratitude Works! A 21-Day Program for Creating Emotional Prosperity*. San Francisco, CA: Jossey-Bass.

If you'd like to read those early dramatic gratitude journaling studies at source, then take a look at:

Emmons, R. A. & McCullough, M. E. (2003). Counting blessings versus burdens: An experimental investigation of gratitude and subjective well-being in daily life. *Journal of Personality and Social Psychology*, 84(2), pages 377–389.

For more information on the links between gratitude and prayer among Christians, you may like to look up the following:

Lambert, N. M., Fincham, F. D., Braithwaite, S. R., Graham, S. M. & Beach, S. R. H. (2009). Can prayer increase gratitude? *Psychology of Religion and Spirituality*, 1(3), pages 139–149.

Rosmarin, D. H., Pirutinsky, S., Cohen, A. B., Galler, Y. & Krumrei, E. J. (2011). Grateful to God or just plain grateful? A comparison of religious and general gratitude. *The Journal of Positive Psychology*, 6(5), pages 389–396.

A complete list of sources is provided in the reference section at the end of the book.

Simple exercises were developed, such as completing a gratitude journal of a few blessings each day, or thinking over a difficult situation with thanks that it hadn't been worse, or imagining the absence of something taken for granted to nurture gratitude for its presence. Even Martin Seligman himself joined the party by designing what must be one of the most powerful gratitude tools. He called it the gratitude visit. It involved identifying those (teachers, parents, mentors, friends) who had never been adequately thanked for the good they had done, writing them a letter of appreciation, and travelling to read it to them in person. For some people this meant nothing more than a quick trip in the car, other people crossed oceans and continents just to read their letters of thanks. The man who famously didn't do gratitude inspired thousands to travel all over the world for the sake of showing they were grateful.[4]

Get Some Exercise!

Gratitude journaling

In terms of regular gratitude practice, journaling is one of the most accessible ways to begin. If you already keep a spiritual journal of some sort, this is an easy addition to your usual practice. A few tips from the literature may help:

Set a regular time to write in your journal – first thing in the morning or last thing at night is usually best.

Many people find that ten to fifteen minutes every other day is the best rhythm of journaling. Some find that more than this can lead to "gratitude fatigue". You can find your own rhythm.

There are different ways to complete a gratitude journal. You can begin by identifying three or four things for which you are grateful each time you write. If you struggle to think of anything, then start by coming up with just one thing. It could be something small, like a sunny day, a smile from a friend, a nice cup of tea, or a favourite TV programme. Any small thing can kick-start gratitude.

The aim is not to write a list, but to try to recall the feelings of gratitude you have towards what you are writing about. Dwell for some minutes on the details of the person or event in question.

To keep your gratitude practice fresh, it's also worth thinking about unusual things you are grateful for. Imagine what your life would be like if some things you took for granted were not there any more, or imagine that things you love are about to come to an end. Use the journal to stretch your gratitude.

Further tips can be found in the references cited in this chapter.

What continues to be surprising about much of this research on gratitude is the incredible benefits reported by those who adopt gratitude practice even for just a few weeks. When subjected to the most rigorous trials, being grateful has been linked to numerous psychological and physical health benefits. Practising thankfulness, to name just a few of the benefits, appears to lead people to be happier, less anxious and less depressed, more physically active with fewer health complaints, less entitled and materialistic, and more spiritually connected.

Shifting the fixed-point of happiness

Gratitude even seems to free us from one of our most stubborn emotional trends. For years the received wisdom in psychology has dictated that we all have a set-point of happiness, a bit like body weight. We can make ourselves happier within limits, but once the pressure is off, we tend to return to our original emotional state. This, it would appear, explains why something that makes us happy today may have lost its sparkle by tomorrow. We adapt to improved circumstances very quickly, the novelty wears off. That which delights us to begin with – the new house, the new car, the new job, the new spouse – may fail even to raise a smile with the passing of time. We get used to what we have and tend to take it for granted.[5]

But not if we're grateful.

Some of the earliest research in gratitude showed that regularly taking ten minutes to revisit things for which we are grateful can have a long-lasting impact on our emotional well-being. In some studies the positive effects of keeping a gratitude journal were still being felt one month, three months, and even as long as six months after the study had drawn to a close. Once people started being grateful they just couldn't stop.[6] Not only did the studies fail to show the familiar dip in happiness that occurs when we get over the novelty of some new good thing in our life but, on the contrary, they seemed to suggest that gratitude is one of the practices that has the potential to shift the fixed-point of happiness in an upward direction.

The reason for this seems to be that when we are grateful we allow ourselves to relive the same good things over and over. Instead of getting used to what we have, we re-present them to ourselves, we enjoy them and are nourished by them. By dwelling on the good gifts of life we receive them time and again, without growing tired of them. It's true that we may experience gratitude fatigue[7] if we trawl our lives too obsessively for things to be thankful for, but on the whole regular gratefulness lifts us off the perpetual treadmill of seeking new things to be happy about. When we are grateful, says Emmons, we take things not *for* granted, but *as* granted.

Thanking is thinking

Mindfulness is therefore frequently aligned with gratitude in the same way that it is often practised with other positive attitudes such as compassion or acceptance. Being grateful requires a moment to pause, to reflect, to appreciate and dwell in the here-and-now. Gratitude is therefore a way of being mindful, a way of thinking about the world. In fact the philosopher Heidegger in describing his own contemplative style of thought was quick to point out that the words "think" and "thank" share a common heritage. He called his philosophy a "thinking that is a thanking", a rich appreciation of the world we have been given. Thanking, he thought, was the best way of thinking.[8]

By the Book

Gratitude in Paul's letters

Perhaps one of the most frequent uses of gratitude in the New Testament, outside of the Gospels, appears in the epistles of Paul.

His letters contain continual expressions of thanks for all kinds of reasons. Nearly fifty verses in the Pauline epistles use terms that can be translated as "thanks". Just to name a few examples: he is thankful for the gospel (e.g. Romans 7:25; 2 Corinthians 9:15), thankful for his co-workers (e.g. Romans 16:4; 2 Timothy 1:3), thankful for other believers (e.g. Ephesians 1:16; 1 Thessalonians 1:2), and thankful for overcoming hardships (e.g. 1 Corinthians 15:57; 2 Corinthians 4:15). Being thankful for other people particularly was a prominent part of Paul's prayer life and he advised others to practise gratitude in like manner (e.g. 1 Thessalonians 5:18; Philippians 4:6; Colossians 3:15) – calling to mind the gifts that God has given them and allowing these to prompt expressions of thanks.

In so doing, Paul offers us a useful way of complimenting and encouraging other believers who have blessed us in some way. By saying we are thankful for them, we recognize the good in them without risking undue flattery that could lead to pride. On several occasions the word translated "thanks" when applied to other people is charis, literally "grace" or "gift". It was Paul's deep appreciation of God's grace that fuelled his perpetual sense of gratitude.

But I suspect most Christians would have some reservations at this point. It's all very well to say that gratitude feels good, or even does us good, but doesn't gratitude also have a deeper dimension than that? Even leading scientists in the field are wary of viewing thankfulness merely as a happiness technique rather than recognizing its status as a complex moral attitude. There is a reason why thanksgiving occupies such a central position in the life of Jesus and lends its name to the most significant ritual of the Christian faith. There is a reason why the apostle Paul litters his letters with expressions of thanks, and commands his recipients to be equally effusive in thanksgiving. There is a reason why Christians ever since have embodied gratitude in spiritual disciplines, exercises, and worship practices of all kinds. The reason is not that gratitude makes us feel good, or even does us good, but because in being grateful we accurately appreciate the way things are. To view the world gratefully is to view the world truly.

The heart of the universe

And that brings us back to hobbits. Or at least to Tolkien's favourite prefix *eu-*, meaning good.

We noted earlier that this is the first part of the Greek word used in the New Testament to denote the act of giving thanks, *eucharisteō*. What we didn't note was that the second part of this word is *charis*, more often translated, when occurring alone, "grace" and often used when Paul thanks God for somebody. It's almost his shorthand for noting that his friends and colleagues were not objects to be used or pawns to be manoeuvred, but precious gifts to be prized and treated royally. Paul delights to take grace, the foundational principle of the good news of Jesus, the very notion that God gave everything he had to the world as a gift, and see it in the people who surrounded him. His gratitude allowed him to look at everyday life and discern a cosmic thread of grace that ran right to the heart of the universe.

In this he follows his master. In the Gospels we read that Jesus takes an everyday packed lunch of bread and fish, and in a simple act of thanks, transforms it into a feast that can feed a crowd. He takes a Passover meal of bread and wine, and in a moment of thanksgiving, communicates a sacrifice that can save the world. When we are grateful we enhance and expand that for which we give thanks. We take friends and food, and in thanking God for them, we invite heaven to breathe life upon them. But more than that, in thanking God for Jesus we enjoy time and again, in ever-increasing richness, the precious and inexhaustible gift of his son.

Being grateful, being mindful

Being grateful to God therefore allows us to know him more fully. Yet for some reason, we need to be reminded of this fact fairly regularly. Research on gratitude helps us to explain the struggles we sometimes have in maintaining a grateful attitude. Because gratitude implies that good things come from outside of ourselves, we may find that we resist acknowledging this. Particularly if we pride ourselves on being self-reliant or independent, we may wish to avoid the notion that we rely all too much on the complex network of life that surrounds us. Furthermore, if we carry a high degree of entitlement, a belief that we deserve good things as our right, or that we've earned them, gratitude will not come naturally to us. Gratitude implies that we've been given so many good things irrespective of whether we deserve them.

This is one of the reasons why mindful contemplation and gratitude make such good companions. For many of us, practising gratitude will require some degree of deprogramming, away from habits of entitlement or selfishness. As Henri Nouwen, the theologian and monk, recognized, the discipline of gratitude was one of the only practices that could free him from habitual feelings of resentment.[9] So too for us, it may be that practising gratitude requires us to pause, to take stock, to look at the world afresh with non-judgmental eyes. In short: being grateful may require us to be mindful.

When Two or Three are Gathered...

Questions for group discussion

You may like to use the following questions to discuss gratitude as a small group.

Reflect for a moment: Who in the group are you grateful for, and for what reason? Spend some time expressing thanks for being gifts to one another.

How grateful would you consider yourself to be in general, and what prevents you from being more consistently thankful?

Talk about some of the more difficult times in your life that you managed to come through. What are you grateful for now that you may have taken for granted before?

When you think of the various ways in which God has loved, supported, and been faithful to you, what comes to mind? How do you feel towards him as a result?

Of the various ways of practising gratitude mentioned in this chapter, are there any that appeal to you as items for regular practice? How, when, and where will you practise them?

Mindful Wisdom

We all live in glasshouses

Over the last few years I have kept a mental list of international experts who are not able to do the very thing that they are experts in. These are people who intellectually speaking know more than any other living person on the planet about a certain area of human behaviour, but are somehow deficient in actually doing what they know.

The longer I have spent in contact with the world of academia, the longer the list has become. It includes the prize-winning expert in face-recognition who cannot identify his own wife on campus; the global guru in conflict management who falls out with everyone; the high-flying memory researcher who forgets everything; and the global genius in authenticity whose CV is full of lies.

Yes... but...

Should Christians be cunning?

Is it right for Christians to be strategic in the way they approach life? Surely, the argument goes, a pure-hearted approach to life reacts innocently and naively to the world, rather than sitting back and mindfully contemplating the best course of action in a way that could be considered artificial or calculating.

The Bible however doesn't draw a distinction between being pure and being thoroughly deliberate in our actions. When Jesus sends his disciples out to spread the good news he tells them to be as innocent as doves and as wise as serpents (Matthew 10:16). The word used for wisdom here is "phronimos" which implies a discreet or cautious mindset. Jesus is saying that, on the one hand, their motives are to be clean and pure, they should deal ethically and respectfully with everyone they meet. On the other hand, they are being sent into a hostile social environment and shouldn't be naive. They need to think carefully as to how and when they speak of Jesus so as to give the message the best chance of being heard.

When Paul writes to the Corinthians of being all things to all people (1 Corinthians 9:22), he is speaking in the same tradition of having pure intentions but adaptable strategies. Living wisely requires both pure motives and clear thinking.

These examples are funny, but others are tragic. Like the respected depression researcher whose daughter committed suicide, or the much-loved child psychologist who was arrested for creating obscene images.

Just because we know something doesn't mean that we can act on it. Just because we know the good we ought to do, doesn't mean we can do it. It is tempting to laugh at it as a folly confined to absent-minded professors, but it extends to all of us. We all live in glasshouses. We all fail to live up to the standards we expect of others. Very few of us fully practise what we preach.

Early in the twentieth century the theologian Dietrich Bonhoeffer recognized that the "best-informed man is not necessarily the wisest. Indeed there is a danger that precisely in the multiplicity of his knowledge he will lose sight of what is essential." He concluded that wisdom was the ability "to recognize the significant in the factual".[1]

When we ask the question, "How then should we live?", we are beginning to seek not just information, but wisdom.

Knowing without doing

The danger of knowing without doing is just as real for Christians as it is for academics.

Most active Christians are bombarded weekly with instruction on living a good life. But this can lead to self-deception. Knowing the New Testament Greek words for love may not mean we are loving. Sitting through a sermon on faith may not mean we are full of faith. This discrepancy between knowing and doing was famously and wonderfully expressed two millennia ago by the apostle Paul in writing to the church in Rome:

> I do not understand what I do. For what I want to do I
> do not do, but what I hate I do. And if I do what I do not
> want to do, I agree that the law is good. As it is, it is no
> longer I myself who do it, but it is sin living in me. For I
> know that good itself does not dwell in me, that is, in my
> sinful nature. For I have the desire to do what is good, but
> I cannot carry it out. For I do not do the good I want to
> do, but the evil I do not want to do – this I keep on doing.
> (Romans 7:15–19)

His colleague James reminds us not just to hear the word of God but to embody it in practice (James 1:22–25). Otherwise, he argues, we run the risk of being like someone who glances at themselves in the mirror but immediately forgets what they've seen when they walk away. We take a good, hard look at ourselves, at all our faults and foibles, and then forget what we've seen in favour of an airbrushed image of our moral lives.

This discrepancy between knowing what to do and knowing how to do it has been pondered by psychologists for some years. Quite a few have bemoaned the fact that Western education has a bias towards teaching us what to know to the neglect of *how to live.* Some have called this educational culture "hyper-cognitive", prizing intellectual performance above all else, and ignoring other forms of intelligence and ability. These other intelligences include social and emotional ability, physical coordination, creative thinking, and ethical discernment. Anyone who leaves school or college feeling that they are a failure or stupid is most probably a victim of this over-focus on IQ.

Interestingly, it is one of the leading researchers of IQ who has been most vocal in acknowledging this deficit. Legendary psychologist, Robert Sternberg of Yale, is one among a number of researchers internationally who have turned their attention towards the development of wisdom.[2] If intelligence tells us what things are, wisdom is the capacity to know what to do with them. When water falls from the sky intelligence tells us that it's rain, wisdom tells us to cover up or get inside. Sternberg developed what he called the balance theory of wisdom and, alongside the understanding of wisdom developed by a team in Berlin,[3] it has become the principal way in which psychologists understand what it means to be wise.

Psychological models of wisdom stress that those who are wise have an expertise in the pragmatics of life. They may indeed have a rich factual knowledge, but this is equalled by a rich procedural knowledge – i.e. knowing how to do things. Wise people tend to see the mundane action of daily life from a wider perspective. They think about how their behaviour and that of others will affect the environment around them in the long term. This means that they are highly attuned to the way in which their values and priorities are put into practice in present decisions. Psychologically speaking, the core of wisdom is the ability to spot and be prepared to work with situations where the outcome is uncertain. Wise people know what to do (even if this means doing nothing), when most of us don't know what to do.

Help... I'm a Geek

Further reading in wisdom

If you want to understand the background to wisdom research, the handbook that covers all the leading thinkers in the psychology of wisdom is:

Sternberg, R. J. & Jordan, J. (eds.). (2005). *A Handbook of Wisdom: Psychological Perspectives.* Cambridge: Cambridge University Press.

The oft-quoted distinction between practical, everyday wisdom and transcendent wisdom is addressed in this slightly older article:

Wink, P. & Helson, R. (1997). Practical and transcendent wisdom: Their nature and some longitudinal findings. *Journal of Adult Development,* 4(1), pages 1–15.

The role that wisdom played in the early church is examined in this article that integrates theological reflection and psychological science:

Collicutt, J. (2006). Post-traumatic growth and the origins of early Christianity. *Mental Health, Religion and Culture,* 9(3), pages 291–306.

For a full statement and critique of the Berlin Wisdom Paradigm, you could take a look at the following:

Banicki, K. (2009). The Berlin wisdom paradigm: A conceptual analysis of a psychological approach to wisdom. *History & Philosophy of Psychology,* 11(2), pages 25–36.

A full list of sources is provided in the reference section at the end of the book.

The beguiling complexity of life is evident when we look at the Hebrew wisdom literature. There are sections in Proverbs where the advice given in one soundbite seems to directly contradict the advice given in another. And it's not as if the editors of the book tried to hide the discrepancy – sometimes the contrasting proverbs are placed right next to each other. In the twenty-sixth chapter of Proverbs, verse four says: "Do not answer a fool according to his folly, or you yourself will be just like him."

Very sage advice. It is important that we don't fall into the trap of arguing fruitlessly with someone entrenched in their own ignorance. A great principle for living.

But then verse five says: "Answer a fool according to his folly, or he will be wise in his own eyes." Again, great advice. We often need to speak up and offer an alternative opinion when faced with the person who loves to hold court while spreading ignorant or ill-informed opinions. It would be wrong to stay silent.

But here's the confusion. When do we do which? Do we answer ignorance or do we stay silent? We are faced with a genuine dilemma in which either response can be appropriate given the right circumstances. Sometimes silence is preferable to the mudslinging that can occur when bigoted opinions are challenged. Sometimes it is morally wrong to remain silent when arrogant or damaging views are expressed.

Wisdom is not just about knowing what we should do, it's about knowing when to do what we should do. The Bible and psychological science are agreed, this is the special expertise that wise people bring to the table. They have an appreciation of paradox. We face many situations where we may not know exactly what to do, and wisdom is what we need to find our way forward.

Where wisdom comes from

We need wisdom because life is confusing. When Paul and James wrote about the need to be wise they were drawing on the Jewish wisdom tradition to which they belonged. The Hebrew word for wisdom used in the Proverbs is *hokma*. It is translated "wisdom", but more fully it means ethical, practical, and spiritual skill. It refers to the ability of an expert craftsman and therefore also to the art of skilful living. Right at the beginning of Proverbs, it is associated with the fear of the Lord:

The fear of the Lord is the beginning of knowledge,
but fools despise wisdom and instruction.
(Proverbs 1:7)

The fear of the Lord is not a relationship with God in which we walk on eggshells, fearing a lightning bolt from heaven. Rather Proverbs 1:7 suggests that wisdom begins with reverential mindfulness of God. To fear God in this case is to live with an awareness of our limitations and fragility as mortals together with our ultimate accountability for how we live. Fearing God diminishes presumptuous and thoughtless action in favour of well-considered, purposeful living. It requires us to bring mindful attention to our everyday lives; to our speech, our thoughts, our actions and reactions.

But it is not an oppressive demand. Many of the proverbs imply a lightness of touch in living. Some of them are voiced in an ironic tone. Humour appears to be an important part of wisdom. It invites us to look at the gap between who we are and who we ought to be, and laugh at the discrepancy. Wise people fear the Lord but still have an appetite for life.

By the Book

Worldly wisdom and godly wisdom

Wisdom is of course a prominent theme in many books of the Old and New Testaments.

In New Testament Greek, the most frequently used root word for wisdom is "sophia", which refers to both the skill and wisdom in managing daily affairs, but also the deeper supreme wisdom of God. This is the word that lies behind the English word "philosophy", literally meaning "the love of wisdom".

The most extended use of sophia and its derivatives occurs in the opening chapters of the first letter to Corinth. Paul is keen to stress the difference between worldly wisdom which rests on the sheer cleverness of manipulating the affairs of life, and God's wisdom which is found in Christ (1 Corinthians 1:24). In terms of the everyday strategic wit that leads to self-advantage, Paul is quick to recognize that Christians may not be recognized for possessing this in abundance (1 Corinthians 1:26). But we are the recipients of a greater wisdom of God, which may look like foolishness in terms of short-term advantages to ourselves, but which belongs to God's long-term plan for Creation. Paul therefore argues that we may have to give up our ability to manipulate those around us for personal gain, if we are to become truly wise in the Christian sense of the word (1 Corinthians 3:18).

The wisdom of God is not just about individuals getting ahead, it seeks the good of the world around us. When we ask God for wisdom this is what we are seeking – the best possible course of action for all.

Psychologists also have debated where wisdom comes from. Is wisdom an average everyday skill that any observant person can learn? Or is it a mystical insight that originates beyond everyday life?[4] This question has been posed about quite a few other things too. Like the meaning of life: do we create it for ourselves or is it out there waiting to be found?[5] Or hope: is it just a way of thinking about things, or does hope somehow connect to the deeper purpose of the universe?[6] The Bible doesn't seem to be that interested in drawing a line between everyday wisdom and divine wisdom. It draws on both. It welcomes the common sense that makes for harmonious daily living, as we see in Proverbs, and at the same time tells us to seek the wisdom of God.

There is one distinction however that the Bible is keen to draw: between *worldly* wisdom and *godly* wisdom. The point at issue here is not whether wisdom arises out of the daily grind or from mystical experience, but whether our wisdom involves scheming for self-promotion, or thoughtful living for others to the glory of God. Worldly wisdom is the Machiavellian cunning that serves selfish ambition. Godly wisdom is the learning that ultimately brings peace with others and with God.

When it comes to wisdom the Bible is rather like one of those epic stories like Homer's *Odyssey* or Tolstoy's *War and Peace*. The nature of an epic is that it tells a huge, sweeping story of global significance, by attending to the small details of the lives of the people involved. An epic tells a big story through small details. And that is in many ways similar to what the Bible does with wisdom. Biblically speaking, wisdom is not only divinely revealed insight, nor is it just the smarts needed to live each day skilfully – it's both.

The opening chapters of Proverbs set out the background against which everyday wisdom should be understood. Not only is wisdom personified as a woman crying out in the streets and marketplaces, it is something much deeper than that. Wisdom does not just drag its feet through the streets calling those with the ears to hear, it is woven like a thread into the fabric of the world around us, it is embedded like a code into the operating system of the world. It is somehow part of Creation. In Proverbs 8:22–31, we read:

> *The Lord brought me forth as the first of his works,*
> *before his deeds of old;*
> *I was formed long ages ago,*
> *at the very beginning, when the world came to be.*
> *When there were no watery depths, I was given birth,*
> *when there were no springs overflowing with water;*
> *before the mountains were settled in place,*
> *before the hills, I was given birth,*
> *before he made the world or its fields*
> *or any of the dust of the earth.*
> *I was there when he set the heavens in place,*
> *when he marked out the horizon on the face of the deep,*

when he established the clouds above
and fixed securely the fountains of the deep,
when he gave the sea its boundary
so the waters would not overstep his command,
and when he marked out the foundations of the earth.
Then I was constantly at his side.
I was filled with delight day after day,
rejoicing always in his presence,
rejoicing in his whole world
and delighting in mankind.

It is undoubtedly this Old Testament passage, and others like it, that lie behind the opening of John's Gospel, in which Jesus is referred to as the Word:

In the beginning was the Word, and the Word was with
God, and the Word was God. He was with God in the
beginning. Through him all things were made; without
him nothing was made that has been made. (John 1:1–3)

Get Some Exercise!

Seeking wisdom

The need for wisdom becomes most apparent when faced with difficult decisions. Whenever we find ourselves asking what we should do, we are asking for wisdom. The following exercise is designed to help you open yourself to the wisdom of God in difficult circumstances.

Recognize that the situation you are facing requires some wisdom. If you keep doing the same thing you will keep getting the same result. This situation, whatever it is, requires something different, and that's where wisdom comes in.

Put some space between you and the stress of the situation that is facing you – take a deep breath, go for a walk, take a moment alone – so that your mind can relax and become receptive to alternative courses of action.

In this receptive state, ask God for wisdom. Accept that this may not come immediately, you may need to ask persistently, but remind yourself that God has promised to answer this request if we consistently present it.

Reflect on the life of Jesus, wondering what he would do in the situation that presents itself. Even if you have been part of creating the difficulties you are in, what would Jesus do, or what would he recommend that you do? Imagine yourself doing it.

If by the end of the exercise you still can't find a way ahead repeat it, and if possible, seek advice from others. Part of wisdom is recognizing when you are out of your depth and need the help of others.

The aim of this exercise is to get out of unhelpfully turning the problem over in your head, and to find a new broader perspective that will help you move forward.

It is well known that the Greek term translated "word" in this passage is "logos". What is not quite so well known is that logos also implies broader concepts such as meaning, logic, wisdom, and structure. In fact, much of Ancient Greek philosophy was viewed as the pursuit of the "logos", the search for the basic structure and rationale of existence which could then tell us how to live. Wisdom in its various forms could tell us what the world was like and how we should therefore live effectively in it. Uncovering the logos would expose the hidden structure of the cosmos, and offer us a way of being that fitted us into the processes of the world seamlessly, like a hand into a glove. The search for the logos was, in a sense, the search for the ultimate meaning in life.

The opening of John's Gospel therefore makes a radical claim; the search for the logos is over. In fact the logos has revealed himself – in the person of Jesus. Wisdom from the Christian point of view therefore is both transcendent and immanent. It is out there, but also in our midst (Luke 17:21). Wisdom stretches to the edges of the universe, but can also be seen in the everyday life of a Galilean peasant, and in those who model themselves upon him. We become wise by being mindful of Jesus when needing wisdom.

Stop and think

We need wisdom because life is confusing, and we often don't know what to do. But how do we become wise? And what, if anything, has mindfulness got to do with it?

Practically speaking, people who make wise decisions seem to have the ability to pause before acting. The pause gives them a chance to choose the most helpful or skilful response to a situation. Wisdom lies in acting intentionally, not impulsively, in tune with our deepest values and commitments. We have a better chance of behaving ethically if we can stop and think, if we take a mindful moment.

Stopping and thinking is now part of psychological treatment for a variety of lifestyle control issues. People who experience addictive cravings towards substances, or violence, or sexuality, often feel they have to satisfy their urges immediately. Stopping to think for a moment can allow them time to find different ways of addressing the desires that lie behind addiction or compulsive action. Most people are familiar with the idea of counting to ten before acting on anger. Mindfulness intensifies this by providing a moment in which we can choose the course of action that is most helpful.[7]

This is sometimes referred to as activating "wise mind".[8] In other words accessing our ability to think clearly about what to do in any given situation. Wise mind helps us make good decisions by combining emotion and reason. Most good decisions use both reason and emotion to the right extent. If we only reason about something, we spin the wheels of our mind. We think furiously. We come up with ideas and possibilities for a way forward. But we may never act – just thinking isn't enough. By the same token, if we operate on our emotions alone we are likely to act impulsively without really weighing up the costs and benefits of our actions. Following our feelings can lead us to act on our short-term desires to the detriment of our long-term interests.

Somewhere between *emotional* mind and *reasonable* mind lies "wise mind"; the ability to take a deep breath and bring together our thoughts and feelings with the aim of acting wisely. This is where even a few seconds of mindful awareness of the present moment can help us. Stopping and taking a breath can make all the difference in whether we follow our immediate impulses or more thoughtfully redirect our course of action.

Look at it this way

Psychologists see a strong connection between wisdom and something they call "perspective"[9] – the ability to see things from more than one point of view. If we can stand back from a situation and see it from a bit of a distance or use our imagination to see it from another angle we are more likely to come up with a creative solution. Seeing things from the point of view of others (even when they are our opponents) is also an important part of making peace – something that Jesus prized very highly (Matthew 5:9). Research into conflict transformation tells us that seeing the other point of view is particularly difficult if we are in the grip of strong emotion, whether that emotion is bad (hatred) or good (righteous anger).

Throughout the history of the church Christians have valued

retreats into the desert, journeying on pilgrimages, or walking labyrinths as a way of opening up the horizon and helping them to return home with fresh eyes. But we don't need to travel physically to gain a sense of perspective. By helping us become for a while detached from strong emotions, the practice of mindfulness "can loosen the ties to the perspectives that bind us".[10] So mindfulness – like wise road safety practice – enables us not only to stop but to look.

Keep calm and carry on

Earlier we acknowledged that it was the apostle James who wrote most forcibly about needing to practise that which we believe. It is therefore not a huge surprise that wisdom is one of the key concerns in his writing. He tells us what to do in those moments when seeking wisdom in the face of painful experiences. He says:

> *If any of you lacks wisdom, you should ask God, who gives generously to all without finding fault, and it will be given to you. But when you ask, you must believe and not doubt, because the one who doubts is like a wave of the sea, blown and tossed by the wind. That person should not expect to receive anything from the Lord. Such a person is double-minded and unstable in all they do. (James 1:5–7)*

He takes the common sense, stop-and-think approach to wisdom, and adds a divine twist. He tells us that if we need wisdom, we can seek it through prayer and that God is waiting eagerly to give it to us. Just as Solomon in the Old Testament delighted God by requesting wisdom rather than wealth or the trappings of power, so too today our request for wisdom delights a God who is all too willing to grant us insight. However, says James, a life of wisdom requires no small amount of persistence.

We don't just ask once. We set our intention to seek wisdom continually. A life of wisdom is not a one-stop shop, but the product of perpetual practice.

Mindfulness of Christ

Another way psychologists have recommended for the development of wisdom is to ask ourselves what a wise person would do faced with our situation.[11] Sometimes we can think of a person we know whom we consider to be wise, or just ask ourselves the question more abstractly. But either way studies have shown that people really do demonstrate more wisdom if they are prepared to consult, even in their own imagination, a wise counsellor or mentor of some sort.

This approach will of course not be unfamiliar to most Christians. Most of us are familiar with the proverb that those who walk with the wise become wise. Wisdom is not the pursuit of a lone individual but is increased by learning as part of a group and seeking advice from others.

In popular terms, this idea of learning to act wisely by consulting a wise person lay behind the fad of WWJD fashion bracelets several years ago. The initials, which contrary to popular opinion did not stand for World Wide Jazz Day, posed a question to the wearer. In difficult situations they were to ask: What Would Jesus Do?

The bracelet was a prompt, a reminder, to be mindful of Christ in everyday life. To stop and think, yes. But also ask a question, not of a fictional wise character, but of the One who is wisdom – Jesus Christ. Wise living comes to those who persistently seek it, who are prepared to stop, think, reflect, and pray. Ultimately it is our mindfulness of Christ that leads to wisdom of action.

When Two or Three are Gathered...

Questions for small group discussion

You may like to use the following questions to discuss mindful wisdom as a small group.

Talk about a situation in life you are facing that requires some wisdom. Where have you recently been uncertain about what to do?

When faced with uncertain situations like this, what is your usual response (e.g. problem-solve, avoid thinking about it, seek advice, pray, etc.)? How does this differ from the ideas on seeking wisdom presented in this chapter?

What is your understanding of the difference between worldly and godly wisdom as covered in James 3:13–18?

Have you ever felt you received wisdom from God in the face of a difficult decision? Tell the group about it.

In a broader sense, over the last few years, what has God taught you about life that you can share with the group?

How do you plan to seek a wise course of action when facing difficult situations in future?

The Mindful Organization

Mindfulness is not just for individuals to practise alone. Over the last few years there has been growing interest in mindfulness in the organizational world. Just as interest has grown in the clinical world concerning mindfulness as a therapeutic approach to depression and psychological problems, so too has interest grown in the organizational world. Here mindfulness has been viewed as a way of improving resilience and performance, and to deal with the challenges of a high-pressure working life.[1] Mindfulness is the latest in a line of approaches, techniques, or systems designed to promote health and well-being in the workplace.

Health and well-being at work

My first job, many years ago, was researching stress in the workplace. Stress had only recently come onto the agenda. As a junior researcher I was asked to cold-call various organizations in an attempt to drum up interest in taking part in our research. I learned very quickly that stress in the workplace was not a neutral topic. The responses I received varied. Some were surprised at being asked if stress existed. "We are all hardworking people," they suggested, "of course we are stressed." They viewed stress as an unavoidable part of the job, perhaps even a badge of office. Others emphatically denied its existence. "We are all competent and therefore there is no stress," they retorted, as if only incompetent people experienced stress. It appeared at first glance that stress was to be either strenuously denied or boasted about.

And yet even all those years ago, it was recognized that stress carried a price tag in terms of the cost of illness and absence. High figures continue to be quoted today, showing that stress is a financial burden on organizations. One recently published paper estimated that stress-related losses equal £370 million for UK employers.[2] The financial reason for improving well-being at work is now well established. If there is higher well-being with accompanying lower stress, lower absence, and higher productivity, the bottom line will benefit – or so the argument suggests.

However, the financial argument was not sufficient in the early days to encourage organizations to take the well-being of their staff really seriously. It took a legal judgment to propel this aspect of organizational life to the top of the agenda. In 1994 an employer was taken to court by an employee, claiming damages for stress. Until that point, the health and safety legislation was clear on the responsibility of employers for the physical well-being of their workforce. The judgment in 1994 moved the goalposts and declared that employers were now responsible for the emotional and psychological well-being of their staff and damages were awarded against the employer.[3]

Unsurprisingly, this ruling galvanized many organizations into action. As a result of my work in the stress field, I received many phone calls asking for help. However, most organizations were asking how they could recruit staff who did not suffer stress at all, rather than how they could deal more effectively with it when it occurred. It was tempting to reply that, if stress-proof employees were wanted, then robots had better be hired. At that time the attention was still on the individual rather than the organization.

By the Book

The body of Christ

When we consider Christian views of organizational structure there is no better starting point than Paul's understanding of the church. He views the vast, diverse community of followers of Jesus as the body of Christ. In 1 Corinthians 12:12–26, he outlines many of the implications of this.

The first is that everyone has a unique contribution to make to the community. As he puts it, "the body is not made up of one part but of many" (verse 14).

Secondly, Paul is keen to point out that this makes each person indispensable in the same way that each part of the body cannot replace another. In verse 21 he states: "The eye cannot say to the hand, 'I don't need you!' And the head cannot say to the feet, 'I don't need you!'" We need one another and the different gifts we bring to the community of faith.

Thirdly, he recognizes that some parts of the body are given more honour and recognition than others, but this does not mean that they are unequal in status (verses 24–26). All are essential.

Awareness of the value and diversity within the community of the church requires something like mindful awareness. A willingness to suspend judgment and see the value in others, which may be different from our own.

Nevertheless, gradually over the years, awareness has grown that stress may not be all the fault of incompetent or weak people, the organization itself might, just might, have a role to play. So alongside stress management training, there was a move in many workplaces to providing support for staff who were experiencing difficulties. I was involved with setting up a scheme that trained peer counsellors in basic counselling skills, who could then be available to provide support for their colleagues. The scheme was greeted with considerable scepticism at senior levels but it worked well. A more popular option was to buy in employee assistance programmes from outside the organization. But whichever route was chosen, there was a collective sigh of relief, the problem of employee well-being was sorted. The organizational duty of care for emotional and psychological well-being was covered. The problem was solved. Except, of course, that it wasn't.

The continuing interest in health and well-being has led to numerous developments over the last few decades: a large annual conference on the subject now convenes annually, several government white papers have been written, and the number of research papers in psychological journals increases monthly. Yet the problem persists.

Madeleine Bunting talks about an "unfinished revolution".[4] She says that a culture of overwork rules our lives with little talk of a collective solution, only a focus on individuals. The implication being that the problem ultimately lies not with individual employees, but with the organization, its culture, its expectations, and its leadership. This is where mindfulness comes in.

Mindfulness and the current organizational agenda

When I first started my career my overwhelming desire was to make organizations fit for human habitation. Madeline Bunting had used the phrase, "humanising the workplace".[5] In reality, many HR professionals, consultants, psychologists, and managers have a genuine commitment to treating people well. Historically there has been a long history of philanthropic factory owners, families like the Cadburys of chocolate fame who set up a village for their workers and provided benefits. Philanthropy has existed throughout industrial and organizational life, often driven by Christian principles. But well-being is not the main focus of most organizations. As Robert Greenleaf put it, organizations exist to get things done.[6] Each organization exists to achieve its own ends, whether providing a service in the public sector, or making a profit for shareholders in the private sector. The workforce or employees of any organization are the means to achieving the organizational goal. The current focus on staff well-being is therefore linked to the need to keep the human resources of the organization working well.[7]

Many organizations now have as part of their values or statement of principles, "our people are our key resource". In today's knowledge-hungry world, it is brain, not brawn, that helps to achieve organizational goals. And, in addition to brainpower, it is energy and heart that will lead to success. So psychological well-being is a key focus for organizations that want to succeed, and mindfulness is increasingly viewed as having a key part to play in this.

As I was writing this, the latest edition of my professional journal landed on the doormat, containing a review of fourteen studies of resilience.[8] Mindfulness techniques were central among the methods used to increase resilience. The benefits of mindfulness in organizational life have also reached a wider audience through the "for Dummies" series. *Mindfulness at Work for Dummies* was published in 2014,[9] outlining some of the key ways that mindfulness can help address many of the current challenges posed in the workplace.

Mental resilience

A key benefit of mindfulness practice is increased mental resilience, the ability to bounce back or recover after an adverse experience or difficulty. As we have seen in previous chapters, mindfulness practice gives back control. It increases our ability to focus on the present moment, to observe and accept the response, and not just be at the mercy of stress. Over time, mindfulness practice can increase awareness of what is likely to cause stress and help us take action in anticipation.[10]

All sorts of negative thoughts crowd our minds and can lead to negative emotions. Stress is often exacerbated by the unnecessary pressure we put on ourselves. We catastrophize, see the worst, expect the worst, and add to the pressure of the workplace by our own self-critical thinking. Mindfulness techniques allow us to be aware of those patterns, and help to increase our acceptance of what is, in the present, without predictions of a dire future. Mindfulness can help reduce self-generated pressure.

When teaching stress management workshops, I often use the phrase, "be kind to yourself", only to be met with blank looks of incomprehension. The biblical injunction to "love your neighbour" seems to be well understood and the need for good interpersonal skills accepted, but the second part of the command, "as yourself", often passes people by. Being kind to self, or self-compassion, is a key benefit of mindfulness practice. At the very least learning how not to be your own harshest critic will help. As research on appraisal systems in organizations has found, managers do not need to point out failings to staff, staff will be only too well aware of them themselves. Learning how to be our best friend, not our own worst enemy, is a key part of mental resilience in the workplace.

Time and work–life balance

As Madeline Bunting explores so well in her book on the overwork culture, *Willing Slaves*,[11] time is a key pressure in the workplace, even going as far as to describe time as the new money. She makes the point that people work very long hours in the UK. As a nation we have a long-hours culture, irrespective of whether long hours always lead to increased productivity. Parents who work often feel the conflict of balancing the demands of a family with the demands of work. It takes a strong-minded and principled individual to set totally clear boundaries around the working day. In many organizations there is a culture that expects work to take priority at all times, even though lip service is frequently paid to work–life balance and family-friendly policy.

Modern technology has made these boundaries even more permeable, as work invades the home thanks to remote email access and online work platforms. But it is not just the technological ability to be at work at all times that causes this, but the pressure that our culture exerts to do so – the culture of our society, and the culture within each organization.

Mindfulness practice increases focus and awareness. Each individual when practising mindfulness can focus on their own priorities, become more aware of what matters to them, and make more grounded decisions about how good work–life balance can be achieved.[12] But even more, mindfulness can help the leaders within organizations become aware of the example they set.

Mindful leadership

In 2001, leadership scholar Jim Collins conducted a large-scale research project into leading businesses, the organizations which had become leaders in their field, according to a variety of criteria.[13] The results were ultimately published in the bestselling book *Good to Great*[14] in which he outlined the features that had led these companies to improve from average performance in the marketplace to exceptional leaders in their field.

One of the findings that came as a great surprise to Collins and his research team was that all of these companies were directed by unusual leaders. They called them "Level 5 Leaders". Leaders who seemed to possess a curious combination of humility with regard to themselves and ambition with regard to their organization. Collins summed this up with regard to their response to success and failure as follows: "[the level five leader] looks in the mirror, not out the window to apportion responsibility for poor results... [the level five leader] looks out the window, not in the mirror, to apportion credit for the success of the company."[15] When failing they reflected on their own contribution to the failure, when succeeding they recognized the contribution of their team. The companies led by these individuals were not only financially successful but also good places to work according to employees.

Collins was not the first to note that humility in leaders creates loyalty and engagement in those who work with them. Robert Greenleaf had previously made a similar point under the guise of "servant leadership"[16] and numerous leadership scholars since have recognized the often-overlooked importance of humility as a trait in leaders. One large-scale study of nearly 1,000 employees across sixty-three private companies based in China demonstrated that perceptions of

CEO humility were highly linked to a culture of empowerment, engagement, and productivity throughout the organization.[17] Another set of studies suggested that expressed humility from a leader brings out the best contributions from those who work with them and thereby leads to higher work engagement and better staff retention.[18] Humble leaders, among many other things, empower those they work with to bring their best to the table.

The link between being mindful and being humble has been recognized for some time.[19] But this connection becomes even more apparent when we start to look at the psychological ingredients that make up humility. There are at least five hallmarks of humility, from a psychological point of view.[20] These are, if you like, the five fingers on the hand of the humble leader.

Firstly, humble people have a stable, secure, accepting sense of identity. Who they are is much bigger than their circumstances. They know what they are about; they are a signpost, not a weathervane. Their sense of identity is deeper and broader and higher and longer than any particular failure, frustration, or tragedy that comes their way. They do not rise and fall based on how accommodating the world has been to their ego. Humility in this sense is very close to a mindful attitude, particularly when we take into account how humble people take in information non-judgmentally.

Humble people have an undistorted view of themselves, they are free from a self-serving bias. This is the second psychological feature of humility. In other words it allows them to escape the tendency most of us fall into, to attribute success to ourselves and failure to everybody else. It's called the fundamental attribution error,[21] and most of us do it. If we do well it was all down to me, thank-you-very-much; if we don't do so well, someone let us down, or the situation wasn't fair – not my fault.

Thirdly, people who are humble are open to new information, even if it's critical or unflattering. This is central to the capacity of humility to transform situations. Humble people are willing to receive and adapt to new information, even when it's not particularly complimentary.

This is why humility is so essential for leaders – it allows them to keep learning. And it is not just for young leaders learning the ropes, it applies at every age and stage of the leadership life cycle. Emerging leaders need humility to remind them that they still don't know what they're doing, so they can develop in response to their mistakes and get to the point of competence. Mature leaders need humility so they don't get stuck in a rut of doing the same things over and over again when the world has changed around them and they need to change up their skill set so they don't derail, becoming irrelevant or obsolete. Senior leaders need humility to remind them that they are not indispensable or immortal and that they will need to embrace the pain of transition and succession if they are to attain a legacy worth speaking of. Humility radically redefines our definition of maturity. Maturity isn't having it all – it's having nothing left to prove, but a lot still to learn.

In many respects this is what lies behind the transformational power of humility. Humble people are growing people. Humble people are learning people. When someone comes to us with something about us that they struggle to love, humility considers to what extent the challenge might be true, and to what extent we might be able to respond. And in that humble moment of reflection marriages are saved, businesses evolve, churches become joyful, schools burst with life.

When our ego doesn't get in the way

There are two further hallmarks of humility which speak of how humble people relate to others: firstly, they have the ability to live beyond themselves by being orientated and focused on other people. People high in humility have the capacity to decentre themselves. Psychologists have called these moments self-forgetfulness, or un-selving: those moments of crystal-clear clarity, when our ego doesn't get in the way of what we are trying to do, when our view of the world isn't fogged up by self-concern. They are typical of mindful awareness.

Help... I'm a Geek

Further reading in mindful organization

For a brief and entertaining overview of the application and benefits of mindfulness in the workplace, you may like to take a look at:

Alidina, S. & Adams, J. (2014). *Mindfulness at Work for Dummies*. Chichester: John Wiley & Sons.

For a perceptive and well-written critique of the overwork culture and its impact on our lives, see:

Bunting, M. (2011). *Willing Slaves: How the Overwork Culture is Ruling Our Lives*. London: HarperCollins UK.

Jim Collins' work on the Level 5 leader, who embodies both organizational ambition and personal humility, is summarized with many other pertinent findings in:

Collins, J. C. (2001a). *Good to Great*. New York: Random House Business.

You can read about and follow the steps of the monastic community life based on the Rule of Benedict in this simple but profound introduction:

Jamison, C. (2006). *Finding Sanctuary: Monastic Steps for Everyday Life*. London: Liturgical Press.

A full list of sources is provided in the reference section at the end of the book.

Humble leaders bring life to the people they work with, because they are not so preoccupied with their own success or status that they miss the beauty and the ability in the people around them.

Furthermore, in relationships, humble people tend to view other people not as inferior or subordinate but as intrinsically valuable. Humble leaders are not just *focused* on others, they also *believe* in others. Humble leaders know that their success is inextricably bound up with those who help them achieve it. And that's why the studies cited above tell us that humble leaders are also compassionate leaders, grateful leaders, patient leaders, and trustworthy leaders. Because it's not all about them.

Those are the five hallmarks of humility: stable identity, accurate view of self, openness to information, orientation to others, and egalitarian attitude. And when you put them all together they result in some of the most delightful and effective leaders we are ever likely to encounter. They are undoubtedly mindful leaders, whose mindful attitude and awareness cascade throughout the organizations they lead.

The mindful organization

For the Christian, when it comes to humble leadership, we can do no better than considering the person of Jesus. In fact Paul the apostle directs us precisely to consider the humility that Jesus possessed as the incarnate Son of God. In Philippians chapter two he writes:

> Do nothing out of selfish ambition or vain conceit. Rather, in humility value others above yourselves, not looking to your own interests but each of you to the interests of the others. In your relationships with one another, have the same mindset as Christ Jesus:

Who, being in very nature God, did not consider equality
with God something to be used to his own advantage;
rather, he made himself nothing by taking the very nature
of a servant, being made in human likeness.
And being found in appearance as a man, he humbled
himself by becoming obedient to death – even death on a
cross! (Philippians 2:3–8)

Some scholars have suggested that the reason Paul cites this hymn of humility to the church at Philippi is because the community was in danger of fracturing. Two important and prominent women in the church (Euodia and Syntyche)[22] had fallen out with one another and their conflict was becoming a threat to the health of the entire community.

The word for humility that Paul uses with regard to Jesus is derived from the Greek noun *tapeinos* – literally meaning "not rising far from the ground". It means not getting above ourselves, being grounded and present without grasping for more. It is close to the simple definition of mindfulness with which we started the book. This humble attitude was obviously an essential part of community life, as far as Paul was concerned. When he writes to the Ephesians, he tells them, "Be completely humble and gentle; be patient, bearing with one another in love. Make every effort to keep the unity of the Spirit through the bond of peace" (Ephesians 4:2–3). This was how a healthy organization was to be built: "speaking the truth in love, we will grow to become in every respect the mature body of him who is the head, that is, Christ. From him the whole body, joined and held together by every supporting ligament, grows and builds itself up in love, as each part does its work" (Ephesians 4:15–16). And moreover, "Get rid of all bitterness, rage and anger, brawling and slander, along with every form of malice. Be kind and compassionate to one another, forgiving each other, just as in Christ God forgave you" (Ephesians 4:31–32).

The community, the organization, that Paul had in mind embodied many of the mindful qualities we have considered over the previous chapters. He encourages kindness, compassion, non-judgment, awareness of one another – all following the example and Spirit of Christ. It was in community that these qualities were developed, and the community depended upon them for its health and survival. It was a mindful organization. Not just an organization of mindful individuals, but an organization that embedded mindfulness in its culture, practices, and behaviours.

Finding sanctuary

In 2005, the television programme *The Monastery* shed light on the relatively unknown world of a Benedictine monastic community. The programme was unexpectedly popular and drew a great deal of public interest. Christopher Jamison, the abbot of Worth Abbey who appeared in the programme, followed it with a book, *Finding Sanctuary: Monastic Steps for Everyday Life*.[23] In it he outlined steps to build sanctuary in everyday life, each one taken from the Benedictine Rule. He speaks of the need for silence, reflection, and hope, and ultimately offers a clear template for a mindful organization.

Unsurprisingly, humility is one of the key lessons from the monastic life. So too is the need to treat one another kindly and with respect. Perhaps the most surprising aspect of monastic life for a contemporary audience is the requirement of obedience. This is not a concept used too often nowadays, especially in the corporate world. But contrary to popular opinion, Jamison argues that obedience and freedom are not opposites, rather the monastic life is distinguished by obedient freedom. Each person has the freedom to choose to be obedient.

This makes sense in the monastic life but does not fit quite so easily with an image of a successful company. And yet, when Jim Collins described the culture of great businesses, he highlighted discipline. A culture of discipline, he noted, was a key distinction between the great companies that lasted and those that did not. His argument, generated in close observation of a secular setting, is very much along the same lines as the argument put forward for the monastic life. He argues that if the members of an organization have discipline then there is little need for bureaucracy and certainly no need for authoritarian leadership. The more mindful an organization becomes, it would appear, the more content we are to belong to it.

When Two or Three are Gathered...

Questions for small group discussion

You may like to use the following questions to discuss organizational mindfulness as a small group.

When you think about the organizations you are part of, whether the workplace, church, or another group, what do you find most stressful about belonging to them?

Where do you currently feel in most need of mental resilience (i.e. the ability to bounce back from challenging situations)? What could you do to increase your resilience?

If, today, you were to do one simple thing to better manage your work–life balance, what would it be?

Who comes to mind when you think of a leader who manages to combine a humble attitude with a clear sense of direction and determination? What do you think of them as a leader?

If the church became more mindful as an organization, how do you think it would be different in its treatment of people?

Epilogue

Over the course of this book, we have attempted to do two things. Firstly, to help you understand what mindfulness is. Secondly, to point you to where mindful awareness can be helpful in living the Christian life.

In the process we hope that we have conveyed that there is nothing to fear in the recent explosion of interest in mindfulness. Christians have been mindful, and have promoted spiritual exercises similar to mindfulness, for millennia. We therefore need not fear to lose our footing in the flood of mindful books and resources that is sweeping through our culture. While it may be packaged at times in ways that are unfamiliar to us, we can draw confidence and courage from the knowledge that we belong to a mindful movement with its roots in Jesus himself.

We can also therefore be curious. We need not shut the doors and turn the locks against what at first glance appears to be an alternative spiritual movement. Instead, we can be discerning about the current vogue of mindfulness. We can take what is helpful and ignore what is not. We can experiment with mindful practice without needing to abandon our faith in Christ.

We can be mindful, and be Christian.

References

Aikens, K. A., Astin, J., Pelletier, K. R., Levanovich, K., Baase, C. M., Park, Y. Y. & Bodnar, C. M. (2014). Mindfulness goes to work: Impact of an online workplace intervention. *Journal of Occupational and Environmental Medicine*, 56(7), pp. 721–731.

Alidina, S. & Adams, J. (2014). *Mindfulness at Work for Dummies*. Chichester: John Wiley & Sons.

Arch, J. J. & Craske, M. G. (2006). Mechanisms of mindfulness: Emotion regulation following a focused breathing induction. *Behaviour Research and Therapy*, 44(12), pp. 1849–1858.

Baltes, B. B., Clarke, M. A. & Chakrabarti, M. (2013). Work-life balance: The roles of work-family conflict and work-family facilitation. In P. A. Linley, S. Harrington & N. Garcea (eds.), *The Oxford Handbook of Positive Psychology and Work* (pp. 201–212). New York: Oxford University Press.

Baltes, P. B. & Staudinger, U. M. (2000). Wisdom: A metaheuristic (pragmatic) to orchestrate mind and virtue toward excellence. *American Psychologist*, 55(1), pp. 122–136.

Banicki, K. (2009). The Berlin wisdom paradigm: A conceptual analysis of a psychological approach to wisdom. *History & Philosophy of Psychology*, 11(2), pp. 25–36.

Barrington-Ward, S. (2007). *The Jesus Prayer*. Oxford: BRF.

Baumeister, R. F., Bratslavsky, E., Finkenauer, C. & Vohs, K. D. (2001). Bad is stronger than good. *Review of General Psychology*, 5(4), pp. 323–370.

Bishop, S. R., Lau, M., Shapiro, S., Carlson, L., Anderson, N. D., Carmody, J., ... Velting, D. (2004). Mindfulness: A proposed operational definition. *Clinical Psychology: Science and Practice*, 11(3), pp. 230–241.

Blakney, R. B. (tr. & ed.). (1941). *Meister Eckhart: A Modern Translation.* New York: Harper & Bros.

Bonhoeffer, D. (1986). *Ethics.* (E. Bethge, ed.). New York: Macmillan.

Brefczynski-Lewis, J., Lutz, A., Schaefer, H., Levinson, D. & Davidson, R. (2007). Neural correlates of attentional expertise in long-term meditation practitioners. *Proceedings of the National Academy of Sciences USA*, 104(27), pp. 11483–11488.

Brown, K. W. & Ryan, R. M. (2003). The benefits of being present: Mindfulness and its role in psychological well-being. *Journal of Personality and Social Psychology*, 84(4), pp. 822–848.

Brown, K. W., Ryan, R. M. & Creswell, J. D. (2007). Mindfulness: Theoretical foundations and evidence for its salutary effects. *Psychological Inquiry*, 18(4), pp. 211–237.

Bunting, M. (2011). *Willing Slaves: How the Overwork Culture is Ruling our Lives.* London: HarperCollins UK.

Burch, V. & Penman, D. (2013). *Mindfulness for Health – a Practical Guide to Relieving Pain, Reducing Stress and Restoring Wellbeing.* London: Piatkus.

Chancellor, J. & Lyubomirsky, S. (2013). Humble beginnings: Current trends, state perspectives, and hallmarks of humility. *Social and Personality Psychology Compass*, 7(11), pp. 819–833.

Childs, B. (1962). *Memory and Tradition in Israel.* London: SCM.

Collicutt, J. (2006). Post-traumatic growth and the origins of early Christianity. *Mental Health, Religion and Culture*, 9(3), pp. 291–306.

Collicutt, J. (2015). *The Psychology of Christian Character Formation.* London: SCM.

Collins, J. C. (2001a). Level 5 leadership: The triumph of humility and fierce resolve. *Harvard Business Review*, January, pp. 66–76.

Collins, J. C. (2001b). *Good to Great.* New York: Random House Business.

Csikszentmihalyi, M. (1990). *Flow: The Psychology of Optimal Experience.* New York: Harper & Row.

Darley, J. & Batson, C. D. (1973). "From Jerusalem to Jericho": A study of situational and dispositional variables in helping behaviour. *Journal of Personality & Social Psychology,* 27(1), pp. 100–108.

de Cámara, L. G. (1556). *Ignatius' Own Story with a Sampling of His Letters.* (W. J. Young, tr. 1956). Chicago, IL: Loyola University Press.

De Mello, A. (1978). *Sadhana: A Way to God – Christian Exercises in Eastern Form.* New York: Bantam Doubleday Dell Publishing Group.

De Waal, E. (1999). *Seeking God: The Way of St. Benedict.* London: Canterbury Press.

De Waal, E. (2012). *Lost in Wonder: Rediscovering the Spiritual Art of Attentiveness.* London: Canterbury Press.

Draper, B. (2016). *Soulfulness: Deepening the Mindful Life.* London: Hodder & Stoughton.

Duff, J. & Collicutt, J. (2006). *Meeting Jesus: Human Responses to a Yearning God.* London: SPCK.

Emmons, R. A. (2007). *Thanks!: How the New Science of Gratitude Can Make You Happier.* New York: Houghton Mifflin.

Emmons, R. A. (2013). *Gratitude Works! A 21-Day Program for Creating Emotional Prosperity.* San Francisco, CA: Jossey-Bass.

Emmons, R. A. & McCullough, M. E. (2003). Counting blessings versus burdens: An experimental investigation of gratitude and subjective well-being in daily life. *Journal of Personality and Social Psychology,* 84(2), pp. 377–389.

Emmons, R. A. & McCullough, M. E. (eds.). (2004). *The Psychology of Gratitude.* Oxford: Oxford University Press.

English, J. (2003). *Spiritual Freedom.* (2nd ed.). Chicago, IL: Loyola University Press.

Farb, N., Segal, Z., Mayberg, H., Bean, J., McKeon, D., Zainab, F. & Anderson, A. (2007). Attending to the present: Mindfulness meditation reveals distinct neural modes of self-reference. *Social Cognitive & Affective Neuroscience,* 2(4), pp. 313–322.

Farias, M. & Wikholm, C. (2015). *The Buddha Pill: Can Meditation Change You?* London: Watkins Publishing.

Farrarons, E. (2015). *The Mindfulness Colouring Book: Anti-stress Art Therapy for Busy People* (Reprints ed.). London: Boxtree.

Feldman, C. & Kuyken, W. (2011). Compassion in the landscape of suffering. *Contemporary Buddhism: An Interdisciplinary Journal,* 12(1), pp. 143–155.

Fjorback, L., Arendt, M., Ørnbøl, E., Fink, P. & Walach, H. (2011). Mindfulness-based stress reduction and mindfulness-based cognitive therapy – a systematic review of randomized controlled trials. *Acta Psychiatrica Scandinavica,* 124(2), pp. 102–119.

Foster, R. (2008). *Celebration of Discipline: The Path to Spiritual Growth.* London: Hodder.

Gaultierre, B. & Gaultierre, K. (1989). *Mistaken Identity.* Grand Rapids, MI: Baker Press.

Gilbert, P. (2010). *The Compassionate Mind.* London: Constable.

Gilbert, P. & Choden. (2015). *Mindful Compassion.* London: Constable & Robinson.

Goodliff, P. (2005). *With Unveiled Face: A Pastoral and Theological Exploration of Shame.* London: Darton, Longman & Todd.

Gortner, E., Rude, S. S. & Pennebaker, J. W. (2006). Benefits of expressive writing in lowering rumination and depressive symptoms. *Behavior Therapy,* 37(3), pp. 292–303.

Graham, B. (2006). *The Journey: How to Live by Faith in an Uncertain World.* Nashville, TN: Nelson.

Greenleaf, R. K. (1998). *The Power of Servant Leadership.* San Francisco, CA: Berrett-Koehler.

Hariri, A., Bookheimer, S. & Mazziotta, J. (2000). Modulating emotional responses: Effects of a neocortical network on the limbic system. *Neuroreport,* 11(1), pp. 43–48.

Harris, R. (2009). *ACT Made Simple.* Oakland, CA: New Harbinger.

Hayes, S. C. (2005). *Get Out of Your Mind & into Your Life.* Oakland, CA: New Harbinger.

Heidegger, M. (1968). *What is Called Thinking?* (J. G. Gray, tr.). London: HarperColllins.

Horrobin, P. & Leavers, G. (Comp.). (1990). *Mission Praise.* London: Marshall Pickering.

Hülsheger, U. R., Alberts, H. J. E. M., Feinholdt, A. & Lang, J. W. B. (2013). Benefits of mindfulness at work: The role of mindfulness in emotion regulation, emotional exhaustion, and job satisfaction. *Journal of Applied Psychology,* 98(2), pp. 310–325.

Jain, S., Shapiro, S. L., Swanick, S., Roesch, S. C., Mills, P. J., Bell, I. & Schwartz, G. E. R. (2007). A randomized controlled trial of mindfulness meditation versus relaxation training: Effects on distress, positive states of mind, rumination, and distraction. *Annals of Behavioral Medicine,* 33(1), pp. 11–21.

Jamison, C. (2006). *Finding Sanctuary: Monastic Steps for Everyday Life.* London: Liturgical Press.

Jarrett, C. (2015). *Great Myths of the Brain.* Oxford: Wiley Blackwell.

Kabat-Zinn, J. (1994). *Wherever You Go, There You are: Mindfulness Meditation in Everyday Life.* New York: Hyperion.

Kabat-Zinn, J. (2003). Mindfulness-based interventions in context: Past, present, and future. *Clinical Psychology: Science and Practice,* 10(2), pp. 144–156.

Kabat-Zinn, J. (2012). *Mindfulness for Life: An Interview with Jon Kabat-Zinn.* DVD. Mill Valley, CA: Psychotherapy.net.

Kabat-Zinn, J. (2013). *Full Catastrophe Living: How to Cope with Stress, Pain and Illness Using Mindfulness Meditation* (Revised ed.). London: Hachette UK.

Kabat-Zinn, J. (2014). *9 Powerful Meditation Tips from Jon Kabat-Zinn.* Retrieved from http://mrsmindfulness.com/9-meditation-tips

Kabat-Zinn, J., Lipworth, L., Burncy, R. & Sellers, W. (1986). Four-year follow-up of a meditation-based program for the self-regulation of chronic pain: Treatment outcomes and compliance. *The Clinical Journal of Pain,* 2(3), pp. 159–173.

Keating, T. (1986). *Open Mind, Open Heart.* London: Continuum.

Kirkpatrick, L. (2004). *Attachment, Evolution, and the Psychology of Religion.* New York: Guilford.

Knabb, J. (2012). Centering prayer as an alternative to mindfulness-based cognitive therapy for depression relapse prevention. *Journal of Religion and Health,* 51(3), pp. 908–924.

Kolb, D. A. (2015). *Experiential Learning: Experience as the Source of Learning and Development.* Upper Saddle River, NJ: Pearson Education.

Kuyken, W., Warren, F. C., Taylor, R. S., Whalley, B., Crane, C., Bondolfi, G., … Dalgleish, T. (2016). Efficacy of mindfulness-based cognitive therapy in prevention of depressive relapse: An individual patient data meta-analysis from randomized trials. *JAMA Psychiatry,* 73(6), pp. 565–574.

Lambert, N. M., Fincham, F. D., Braithwaite, S. R., Graham, S. M. & Beach, S. R. H. (2009). Can prayer increase gratitude? *Psychology of Religion and Spirituality,* 1(3), pp. 139–149.

Lambert, S. (2016). *Putting on the Wakeful One: Attuning to the Spirit of Jesus Through Watchfulness.* Watford: Instant Apostle.

Langer, E. J. (1989). *Mindfulness.* Boston, MA: De Capo Press.

Lewis, C. S. (1942). *The Screwtape Letters.* Grand Rapids, MI: Zondervan.

Lewis, C. S. (1947). *The Abolition of Man: How Education Develops Man's Sense of Morality.* New York: Macmillan.

Lewis, C. S. (1950). *The Lion, the Witch and the Wardrobe: A Story for Children.* London: Geoffrey Bles.

Lewis, C. S. (1961). *A Grief Observed.* Grand Rapids, MI: Zondervan.

Lewis, C. S. (1963). *Letters to Malcolm: Chiefly on Prayer.* London: Houghton Mifflin Harcourt.

Lewis, S. (2011). *Positive Psychology at Work: How Positive Leadership and Appreciative Inquiry Create Inspiring Organizations.* Chichester: Wiley-Blackwell.

Lieberman, M., Eisenberger, N., Crockett, M., Tom, S., Pfeifer, J. & Way, B. (2007). Putting feelings into words: Affect labeling disrupts amygdala activity in response to affective stimuli. *Psychological Science,* 18(5), pp. 421–428.

Linehan, M. M. (1993a). *Cognitive-behavioral Treatment of Borderline Personality Disorder.* New York: Guilford Press.

Linehan, M. M. (1993b). *Skills Training Manual for Treating Borderline Personality Disorder.* New York: Guilford Press.

Linn, D., Linn S. F. & Linn, M. (1995). *Sleeping with Bread: Holding What Gives You Life.* Mahwah, NJ: Paulist Press.

Lonsdale, D. (1990). *Eyes to See, Ears to Hear: An Introduction to Ignatian Spirituality*. London: Darton, Longman & Todd.

Louth, A. (2013). *Introducing Eastern Orthodox Theology*. London: SPCK.

MAPPG. (2016). *Mindful Nation, UK: Report by the Mindfulness All-Party Parliamentary Group (MAPPG)*. The Mindfulness Initiative.

McCullough, D. (2014). *Silence: A Christian History*. London: Penguin.

McGilchrist, I. (2009). *The Master and His Emissary: The Divided Brain and the Making of the Western World*. New Haven, CT: Yale University Press.

McGrath, R. E. (2015). Character strengths in 75 nations: An update. *The Journal of Positive Psychology*, 10(1), pp. 41–52.

Mikulincer, M., Shaver, P. R. & Pereg, D. (2003). Attachment theory and affect regulation: The dynamics, development, and cognitive consequences of attachment-related strategies. *Motivation and Emotion*, 27(2), pp. 77–102.

Muldoon, T. (2004). *The Ignatian Workout: Daily Spiritual Exercises for a Healthy Faith*. Chicago, IL: Loyola Press.

Neff, K. (2011). *Self Compassion. Stop Beating Yourself Up and Leave Insecurity Behind*. London: Hodder & Stoughton.

Nickerson, R. S. (1998). Confirmation bias: A ubiquitous phenomenon in many guises. *Review of General Psychology*, 2(2), pp. 175–220.

Niemiec, R. M. (2013). VIA character strengths: Research and practice (the first 10 years). In H. H. Knoop & A. Delle Fave (eds.), *Well-being and Cultures: Perspectives on Positive Psychology* (pp. 11–30). New York: Springer.

Niemiec, R. M. (2014). *Mindfulness and Character Strengths: A Practical Guide to Flourishing*. Boston, MA: Hogrefe.

Niemiec, R. M., Rashid, T. & Spinella, M. (2012). Strong mindfulness: Integrating mindfulness and character strengths. *Journal of Mental Health Counseling*, 34(3), pp. 240–253.

Nouwen, H. (1992). *The Return of the Prodigal Son*. London: Darton, Longman & Todd.

Ou, A. Y., Tsui, A. S., Kinicki, A. J., Waldman, D. A., Xiao, Z. & Song, L. J. (2014). Humble chief executive officers' connections to top management team integration and middle managers' responses. *Administrative Science Quarterly*, 59(1), pp. 34–72.

Owens, B. P., Johnson, M. D. & Mitchell, T. R. (2013). Expressed humility in organizations: Implications for performance, teams, and leadership. *Organization Science*, 24(5), pp. 1517–1538.

Painter, C. V. (2012). *Lectio Divina: The Sacred Art*. London: SPCK.

Park, N., Peterson, C. & Seligman, M. E. P. (2004). Strengths of character and well-being. *Journal of Social and Clinical Psychology*, 23(5), pp. 603–619.

Persson, A. (2010). *The Circle of Love: Praying with Rublev's Icon of the Trinity*. Oxford: BRF.

Peters, E. (tr.). (2012). *The Way of Perfection, by Teresa of Avila*. Mineola, NY: Dover.

Peterson, C. & Seligman, M. E. P. (2004). *Character Strengths and Virtues: A Handbook and Classification*. Oxford: Oxford University Press.

Powell, B., Cooper, G., Hoffman, K. & Marvin, B. (2013). *The Circle of Security Intervention. Enhancing Attachment in Early Parent–Child Relationships*. New York: Guilford Press.

Puhl, L. J. (1952). *The Spiritual Exercises of St Ignatius: Based on Studies in the Language of the Autograph*. Chicago, IL: Loyola University Press.

Rashid, T. & Ajum, A. (2014). *Ways to Use VIA Character Strengths*. Retrieved from www.viacharacter.org/resources/ways-to-use-via-character-strengths

Rizzuto, A.-M. (1979). *The Birth of the Living God: A Psychoanalytic Study*. Chicago, IL: Chicago University Press.

Robertson, I. T., Cooper, C. L., Sarkar, M. & Curran, T. (2015). Resilience training in the workplace from 2003 to 2014: A systematic review. *Journal of Occupational and Organizational Psychology*, 88(3), pp. 533–562.

Rosmarin, D. H., Pirutinsky, S., Cohen, A. B., Galler, Y. & Krumrei, E. J. (2011). Grateful to God or just plain grateful? A comparison of religious and general gratitude. *The Journal of Positive Psychology*, 6(5), pp. 389–396.

Ross, L. D. (1977). The intuitive psychologist and his shortcomings: Distortions in the attribution process. In L. Berkowitz (ed.), *Advances in Experimental Social Psychology* (Vol. 10, pp. 174–221). New York: Academic Press.

Rothschild, B. (2000). *The Body Remembers: The Psychophysiology of Trauma and Trauma Treatment*. New York: Norton Professional Books.

Scioli, A. & Biller, H. B. (2009). *Hope in the Age of Anxiety*. Oxford: Oxford University Press.

Segal, Z. V., Williams, J. M. G. & Teasdale, J. D. (2002). *Mindfulness-based Cognitive Therapy for Depression: A New Approach to Preventing Relapse*. New York: Guilford Press.

Seligman, M. E. P., Steen, T. A., Park, N. & Peterson, C. (2005). Positive psychology progress: Empirical validation of interventions. *American Psychologist*, 60(5), pp. 410–421.

Shapiro, S. & Carlson, L. (2009). *The Art and Science of Mindfulness: Integrating Mindfulness into Psychology and the Helping Professions*. Washington, DC: American Psychological Association.

Shaver, P. R., Lavy, S., Saron, C. D. & Mikulincer, M. (2007). Social foundations of the capacity for mindfulness: An attachment perspective. *Psychological Inquiry*, 18(4), pp. 264–271.

Sheldon, K. M. & Lyubomirsky, S. (2006). How to increase and sustain positive emotion: The effects of expressing gratitude and visualizing best possible selves. *The Journal of Positive Psychology*, 1(2), pp. 73–82.

Sheldon, K. M. & Lyubomirsky, S. (2012). The challenge of staying happier: Testing the hedonic adaptation prevention model. *Personality & Social Psychology Bulletin,* 38(5), pp. 670–680.

Siegel, D. J. (2007). *The Mindful Brain: Reflection and Attunement in the Cultivation of Well-being.* New York: W. W. Norton.

Siegel, D. (2010). *Mindsight. Transform Your Brain with the New Science of Kindness.* Oxford: Oneworld.

Snyder, C. R. (1994). *The Psychology of Hope: You Can Get There from Here.* New York: Free Press.

Sperduti, M., Martinelli, P. & Piolino, P. (2012). Neurocognitive model of meditation based on activation likelihood estimation (ALE) meta-analysis. *Consciousness & Cognition,* 21(1), pp. 269–276.

Stahl, B. & Goldstein, E. (2010). *A Mindfulness-based Stress Reduction Workbook.* Oakland, CA: New Harbinger Publications.

Stead, T. (2016). *Mindfulness and Christian Spirituality: Making Space for God.* London: SPCK.

Stein, D., Ives-Deliper, I. V. & Thomas, K. (2008). Psychobiology of mindfulness. *CNS Spectrums,* 13(9), pp. 752–756.

Steindl-Rast, D. (2004). Gratitude as thankfulness and as gratefulness. In R. A. Emmons (ed.), *The Psychology of Gratitude* (pp. 282–289). New York, NY: Oxford University Press.

Sternberg, R. J. & Jordan, J. (eds.). (2005). *A Handbook of Wisdom: Psychological Perspectives.* Cambridge: Cambridge University Press.

Sternberg, R. J., Reznitskaya, A. & Jarvin, L. (2007). Teaching for wisdom: What matters is not just what students know, but how they use it. *London Review of Education,* 5(2), pp. 143–158.

Sundararajan, L. (2005). Happiness donut: A Confucian critique of positive psychology. *Journal of Theoretical and Philosophical Psychology,* 25(1), pp. 35–60.

Swinton, J. (2012). *Dementia: Living in the Memories of God*. London: SCM.

Symington, S. H. & Symington, M. F. (2012). A Christian model of mindfulness: Using mindfulness principles to support psychological well-being, value-based behaviour, and the Christian spiritual journey. *Journal of Psychology and Christianity*, 31(1), pp. 71–77.

Tang, Y., Holzel, B. & Posner, M. (2015). The neuroscience of mindfulness meditation. *Nature Reviews: Neuroscience*, 16, pp. 213–225.

Tang, Y., Lu, Q., Geng, X., Stein, E., Yang, Y. & Posner, M. (2010). Short-term meditation induces white matter changes in the anterior cingulate. *Proceedings of the National Academy of Sciences USA*, 107(35), pp. 15649–15652.

Tang, Y., Rothbart, M., & Posner, M. (2012). Neural correlates of establishing, maintaining and switching brain states. *Trends in Cognitive Science*, 16(6), pp. 330–337.

Teasdale, J. & Barnard, P. (1993). *Affect, Cognition and Change: Re-modelling Depressive Thought*. Hove: Lawrence Erlbaum.

Thomas, R. S. (1975). *Laboratories of the Spirit*. London: Macmillan.

Thorne, B. (2003). *Infinitely Beloved*. London: Darton, Longman & Todd.

Tickle, P. (2001–6). *The Divine Hours*. New York: Doubleday.

Tomlin, G. (2009). *Spiritual Fitness*. London: Continuum.

Tozer, A. W. (1948). *The Pursuit of God*. London: Lakeland.

Trinder, H. & Salkovskis, P. M. (1994). Personally relevant intrusions outside the laboratory: Long-term suppression increases intrusion. *Behaviour Research & Therapy*, 32(8), pp. 833–842.

Van der Kolk, B. (2015). *The Body Keeps the Score: Brain, Mind, and Body in the Healing of Trauma*. London: Penguin.

Vanstone, W. (1982). *The Stature of Waiting*. London: Darton, Longman & Todd.

Vermetten, E. & Bremner, J. (2004). Functional brain imaging and the induction of traumatic recall: A cross-correlational review between neuroimaging and hypnosis. *International Journal of Clinical and Experimental Hypnosis*, 52(3), pp. 280–312.

Watts, F. (ed.). (2007). *Jesus and Psychology.* London: Darton, Longman & Todd.

Welch, S. (2016). *How to Be a Mindful Christian: 40 Simple Spiritual Practices.* Norwich: Canterbury Press.

Williams, J. M. G. & Penman, D. (2011). *Mindfulness: A Practical Guide to Finding Peace in a Frantic World.* London: Piatkus.

Williams, R. (2004). *Silence and Honeycakes: The Wisdom of the Desert.* Oxford: Lion.

Wink, P. & Helson, R. (1997). Practical and transcendent wisdom: Their nature and some longitudinal findings. *Journal of Adult Development,* 4(1), pp. 1–15.

Wong, P. T. P. (ed.). (2012). *The Human Quest for Meaning* (2nd ed.). New York: Routledge.

Wright, N. T. (2010). *Virtue Reborn.* London: SPCK.

Wright, T. A. (2013). More than meets the eye: The role of employee well-being in organizational research. In P. A. Linley, S. Harrington & N. Garcea (eds.), *The Oxford Handbook of Positive Psychology and Work* (pp. 143–154). New York: Oxford University Press.

Zahl, B. P. & Gibson, N. (2012). God representations, attachment to God, and satisfaction with life: A comparison of doctrinal and experiential representations of God in Christian young adults [Special issue]. *International Journal for the Psychology of Religion,* 22(3), pp. 216–230.

Notes

Mindfulness: What's All the Fuss About?

1. MAPPG. (2016). *Mindful Nation UK: Report by the Mindfulness All-Party Parliamentary Group (MAPPG)*. The Mindfulness Initiative.

2. For a meta-analysis of outcome research on depression relapse see, Kuyken, W., Warren, F. C., Taylor, R. S., Whalley, B., Crane, C., Bondolfi, G., ... Dalgleish, T. (2016). Efficacy of mindfulness-based cognitive therapy in prevention of depressive relapse: An individual patient data meta-analysis from randomized trials. *JAMA Psychiatry*, 73(6), pages 565–574.

3. For a review of the two main evidence-based mindfulness programmes see, Fjorback, L., Arendt, M., Ørnbøl, E., Fink, P. & Walach, H. (2011). Mindfulness-based stress reduction and mindfulness-based cognitive therapy: a systematic review of randomized controlled trials. *Acta Psychiatrica Scandinavica*, 124(2), pages 102–119.

4. A short synopsis of these findings is offered in Williams, J. M. G. & Penman, D. (2011). *Mindfulness: A Practical Guide to Finding Peace in a Frantic World*. London: Piatkus.

5. See Farias, M. & Wikholm, C. (2015). *The Buddha Pill: Can Meditation Change You?* London: Watkins Publishing.

6. For the most recent edition, see Kabat-Zinn, J. (2013). *Full Catastrophe Living: How to Cope with Stress, Pain and Illness Using Mindfulness Meditation* (Revised ed.). London: Hachette UK.

7. Kabat-Zinn, J. (1994). *Wherever You Go, There You are: Mindfulness Meditation in Everyday Life.* New York: Hyperion, page 4.

8. Bishop, S. R., Lau, M., Shapiro, S., Carlson, L., Anderson, N. D., Carmody, J., ... Velting, D. (2004). Mindfulness: A proposed operational definition. *Clinical Psychology: Science and Practice,* 11(3), pages 230–241.

The Mindful Person

1. Shapiro, S. & Carlson, L. (2009). *The Art and Science of Mindfulness: Integrating Mindfulness into Psychology and the Helping Professions.* Washington, DC: American Psychological Association.

2. Brown, K. W., Ryan, R. M. & Creswell, J. D. (2007). Mindfulness: Theoretical foundations and evidence for its salutary effects. *Psychological Inquiry,* 18(4), pages 211–237.

3. Kabat-Zinn, J. (2014). *9 Powerful Meditation Tips from Jon Kabat-Zinn.* Retrieved from www.mrsmindfulness.com/9-meditation-tips

4. Gilbert, P. & Choden. (2015). *Mindful Compassion.* London: Robinson, page 306.

5. Collicutt, J. (2015). *The Psychology of Christian Character Formation.* London: SCM, page 136.

6. Feldman, C. & Kuyken, W. (2011). Compassion in the landscape of suffering. *Contemporary Buddhism: An Interdisciplinary Journal,* 12(1), pages 143–155, page 145.

7. Collicutt (2015), page 137.

8. Siegel, D. J. (2007). *The Mindful Brain: Reflection and Attunement in the Cultivation of Well-being.* New York: W. W. Norton.

9. Stahl, B. & Goldstein, E. (2010). *A Mindfulness-based Stress Reduction Workbook.* Oakland, CA: New Harbinger Publications.

10. e.g. Kabat-Zinn, J., Lipworth, L., Burncy, R. & Sellers, W. (1986). Four-year follow-up of a meditation-based program for the self-regulation

of chronic pain: Treatment outcomes and compliance. *The Clinical Journal of Pain,* 2(3), pages 159–173.

11. Ibid.

12. For example see Stein, D., Ives-Deliper, I. V. & Thomas, K. (2008). Psychobiology of mindfulness. *CNS Spectrums,* 13(9), pages 752–756, or Vermetten, E. & Bremner, J. (2004). Functional brain imaging and the induction of traumatic recall: A cross-correlational review between neuroimaging and hypnosis. *International Journal of Clinical and Experimental Hypnosis,* 52(3), pages 280–312.

13. The best way of testing this is to carry out a longitudinal study, following up novice meditators from a pre-training baseline; but there are very few of these, see Tang, Y., Holzel, B. & Posner, M. (2015). The neuroscience of mindfulness meditation. *Nature Reviews: Neuroscience,* 16, pages 213–225.

14. Lieberman, M., Eisenberger, N., Crockett, M., Tom, S., Pfeifer, J. & Way, B. (2007). Putting feelings into words: Affect labelling disrupts amygdala activity in response to affective stimuli. *Psychological Science,* 18(5), pages 421–428.

15. Hariri, A., Bookheimer, S. & Mazziotta, J. (2000). Modulating emotional responses: Effects of a neocortical network on the limbic system. *Neuroreport,* 11(1), pages 43–48.

16. Brefczynski-Lewis, J., Lutz, A., Schaefer, H., Levinson, D. & Davidson, R. (2007). Neural correlates of attentional expertise in long-term meditation practitioners. *Proceedings of the National Academy of Sciences USA,* 104(27), pages 11483–11488; Tang, Y., Lu, Q., Geng, X., Stein, E., Yang, Y. & Posner, M. (2010). Short-term meditation induces white matter changes in the anterior cingulate. *Proceedings of the National Academy of Sciences USA,* 107(35), pages 15649–15652.

17. Farb, N., Segal, Z., Mayberg, H., Bean, J., McKeon, D., Zainab, F. & Anderson, A. (2007). Attending to the present: Mindfulness meditation reveals distinct neural modes of self-reference. *Social Cognitive & Affective Neuroscience,* 2(4), pages 313–322.

18. Siegel, D. J. (2007).

19. Tang, Y., Rothbart, M. & Posner, M. (2012). Neural correlates of establishing, maintaining and switching brain states. *Trends in Cognitive Science,* 16(6), pages 330–337; Sperduti, M., Martinelli, P. & Piolino, P. (2012). Neurocognitive model of meditation based on activation likelihood estimation (ALE) meta-analysis. *Consciousness & Cognition,* 21(1), pages 269–276.

The Mindful Christian

1. Darley, J. & Batson, C. D. (1973). "From Jerusalem to Jericho": A study of situational and dispositional variables in helping behaviour. *Journal of Personality & Social Psychology,* 27(1), pages 100–108.

2. This passage uses the word *zākar*, which we have seen means to "be mindful". Psalm 1 uses the word *hāgâ* which has overtones of speaking or chanting. In Psalm 63:6 the two verbs form a parallelism, which indicates that their meaning is closely connected. Both can be translated "meditate".

3. This was definitely used in the 300s and almost certainly dates back to the first century after Christ.

4. Peters, E. (tr.). (2012). *The Way of Perfection, by Teresa of Avila.* Mineola, NY: Dover.

5. Blakney, R. B. (tr. & ed.). (1941). *Meister Eckhart: A Modern Translation.* New York: Harper & Bros, page 9.

6. Thomas, R. S. (1975). *Laboratories of the Spirit.* London: Macmillan, page 60.

7. "He said to them, 'Therefore every teacher of the law who has become a disciple in the kingdom of heaven is like the owner of a house who brings out of his storeroom new treasures as well as old'" (Matthew 13:52).

8. See "By the Book" box, page 61.

9. Knabb, J. (2012). Centering prayer as an alternative to mindfulness-based cognitive therapy for depression relapse prevention. *Journal of Religion and Health,* 51(3), pages 908–924.

10. Examples of recommended sacred words are "Jesus", "Spirit", "Abba", "amen", "open", "glory". The sacred word does not refer to anything (otherwise it too might become an idol); it is simply a fitting way of supporting reorientation to the God who is beyond words. It is used flexibly and may be discarded when it becomes unnecessary.

Turning to the Compassionate God

1. Zahl, B. P. & Gibson, N. (2012). God representations, attachment to God, and satisfaction with life: A comparison of doctrinal and experiential representations of God in Christian young adults [Special issue]. *International Journal for the Psychology of Religion,* 22(3), pages 216–230.

2. Powell, B., Cooper, G., Hoffman, K. & Marvin, B. (2013). *The Circle of Security Intervention. Enhancing Attachment in Early Parent–Child Relationships.* New York: Guilford Press.

3. Ibid.

4. Mikulincer, M., Shaver, P. R. & Pereg, D. (2003). Attachment theory and affect regulation: The dynamics, development, and cognitive consequences of attachment-related strategies. *Motivation and Emotion,* 27(2), pages 77–102, page 80.

5. Lewis, C. S. (1942). *The Screwtape Letters.* Grand Rapids, MI: Zondervan, page 47.

6. Shaver, P. R., Lavy, S., Saron, C. D. & Mikulincer, M. (2007). Social foundations of the capacity for mindfulness: An attachment perspective. *Psychological Inquiry,* 18(4), pages 264–271, page 267.

7. Ibid., page 29.

8. Feldman, C. & Kuyken, W. (2011). Compassion in the landscape of suffering. *Contemporary Buddhism: An Interdisciplinary Journal*, 12(1), pages 143–155, page 145.

9. Ibid., page 148.

10. For more details see https://staldates.org.uk/courses/encounter

11. Gaultierre, B. & Gaultierre, K. (1989). *Mistaken Identity*. Grand Rapids, MI: Baker Press.

12. Lewis, C. S. (1950). *The Lion, the Witch and the Wardrobe: A Story for Children*. London: Geoffrey Bles.

13. Lewis, C. S. (1961). *A Grief Observed*. Grand Rapids, MI: Zondervan, page 55.

14. C. S. Lewis (1950).

Turning Inward with Eyes to See

1. Lewis, C. S. (1963). *Letters to Malcolm: Chiefly on Prayer*. London: Houghton Mifflin Harcourt.

2. Brown, K. W., Ryan, R. M. & Creswell, J. D. (2007). Mindfulness: Theoretical foundations and evidence for its salutary effects. *Psychological Inquiry*, 18(4), pages 211–237, here page 213.

3. Siegel, D. J. (2007). *The Mindful Brain: Reflection and Attunement in the Cultivation of Well-being*. New York: W. W. Norton, page 92.

4. Brown, K. W. & Ryan, R. M. (2003). The benefits of being present: Mindfulness and its role in psychological well-being. *Journal of Personality and Social Psychology*, 84(4), pages 822–848, here page 844.

5. Neff, K. (2011). *Self Compassion. Stop Beating Yourself up and Leave Insecurity Behind*. London: Hodder & Stoughton, page 113.

6. Trinder, H. & Salkovskis, P. M. (1994). Personally relevant intrusions outside the laboratory: Long-term suppression increases intrusion. *Behaviour Research & Therapy*, 32(8), pages 833–842.

7. Lewis, C. S. (1963), pages 20–21.

8. The psychiatrist Ian McGilchrist explores this aspect of the Western church in his widely read 2009 book, *The Master and His Emissary* (New Haven, CT: Yale University Press), for example on page 441. It is a helpful piece of historical and cultural analysis, but the claims it makes about brain science should be treated with caution (see Jarrett, C. (2015). *Great Myths of the Brain*. Oxford: Wiley Blackwell).

9. Teasdale, J. & Barnard, P. (1993). *Affect, Cognition and Change: Re-modelling Depressive Thought*. Hove: Lawrence Erlbaum.

Turning Towards Pain and Need

1. Acceptance and Commitment Therapy (ACT) uses many of the principles of mindfulness as a means of enabling the client to commit to positive life change by setting goals that originate in her own values rather than those that have been imposed externally. It talks of seeing that a person can separate themselves from "self as context" to describe adopting the vantage point of just witnessing or noticing. See Harris, R. (2009). *ACT Made Simple*. Oakland, CA: New Harbinger.

2. Williams, J. M. G. & Penman, D. (2011). *Mindfulness: A Practical Guide to Finding Peace in a Frantic World*. London: Piatkus, page 48.

3. Burch, V. & Penman, D. (2013). *Mindfulness for Health – A Practical Guide to Relieving Pain, Reducing Stress and Restoring Wellbeing*. London: Piatkus, pages 3–5.

4. See Burch, V. & Penman, D. (2013). Week 6 "The Tender Gravity of Kindness", pages 177–197.

5. Hayes, S. C. (2005). *Get Out of Your Mind & into Your Life*. Oakland, CA: New Harbinger, pages 153–164.

6. Symington, S. H. & Symington, M. F. (2012). A Christian model of mindfulness: Using mindfulness principles to support psychological well-being, value-based behaviour, and the Christian spiritual journey. *Journal of Psychology and Christianity*, 31(1), pages 71–77.

7. Siegel, D. J. (2007). *The Mindful Brain: Reflection and Attunement in the Cultivation of Well-being.* New York: W. W. Norton, pages 122–123.

8. My italics.

9. Langer, E. J. (1989). *Mindfulness.* Boston, MA: De Capo Press, page 201.

10. Ibid., page 201.

Mindful Bible Reading

1. For an example see, Farrarons, E. (2015). *The Mindfulness Colouring Book: Anti-stress Art Therapy for Busy People* (Reprints ed.). London: Boxtree.

2. James Pennebaker and his colleagues have been investigating the benefits of expressive writing for several decades, see for example, Gortner, E., Rude, S. S. & Pennebaker, J. W. (2006). Benefits of expressive writing in lowering rumination and depressive symptoms. *Behavior Therapy,* 37(3), pages 292–303.

3. For a review, see Nickerson, R. S. (1998). Confirmation bias: A ubiquitous phenomenon in many guises. *Review of General Psychology,* 2(2), pages 175–220.

4. For an example of the effect of mindfulness on depressive rumination see, Jain, S., Shapiro, S. L., Swanick, S., Roesch, S. C., Mills, P. J., Bell, I. & Schwartz, G. E. R. (2007). A randomized controlled trial of mindfulness meditation versus relaxation training: Effects on distress, positive states of mind, rumination, and distraction. *Annals of Behavioral Medicine,* 33(1), pages 11–21.

5. Extensively covered in Segal, Z. V., Williams, J. M. G. & Teasdale, J. D. (2002). *Mindfulness-based Cognitive Therapy for Depression: A New Approach to Preventing Relapse.* New York: Guilford Press.

6. An expression used in Williams, J. M. G. & Penman, D. (2011). *Mindfulness: A Practical Guide to Finding Peace in a Frantic World.* London: Piatkus.

Mindful Reflection

1. Alexander, C. F. (1848). All things bright and beautiful. In P. Horrobin and G. Leavers (Comp.) (1990), *Mission Praise* (number 23). London: Marshall Pickering.

2. de Cámara, L. G. (1556). *Ignatius' Own Story with a Sampling of his Letters.* (W. J. Young, tr. 1956). Chicago, IL: Loyola University Press, pages 7–12.

3. Ibid., page 9.

4. Ibid., pages 7–12.

5. Ibid., page 7.

6. Ibid., page 7.

7. Ibid., page 22.

8. Ibid., pages 17–27.

9. Lonsdale, D. (1990). *Eyes to See, Ears to Hear: An Introduction to Ignatian Spirituality.* London: Darton, Longman & Todd, page 28.

10. Kolb, D. A. (2015). *Experiential Learning: Experience as the Source of Learning and Development* (2nd ed.). Upper Saddle River, NJ: Pearson Education, page 49.

11. Ibid., page 51.

12. Ibid., page 197.

13. Dewey cited in Kolb (2015), page 197.

14. Ibid., page 336.

15. De Camara (1556), page 41.

16. Puhl, L. J. (1952). *The Spiritual Exercises of St Ignatius: Based on Studies in the Language of the Autograph.* Chicago, IL: Loyola University Press, page 1.

17. Tomlin, G. (2009). *Spiritual Fitness*. London: Continuum.

18. Ibid.

19. Lonsdale (1990), pages 69–76.

20. In many Christian traditions a formal accountability relationship is established with a "soul friend" or "spiritual director".

21. This Examination of Consciousness differs from the Examination of Conscience that appears in two forms within the text of the Spiritual Exercises, which is more concerned with issues of morality in an individual's life (see Puhl, 1952, pages 15–23).

22. Muldoon, T. (2004). *The Ignatian Workout: Daily Spiritual Exercises for a Healthy Faith*. Chicago, IL: Loyola Press, page 35.

23. Ibid., page 38.

24. Linn, D., Linn, S. F. & Linn, M. (1995). *Sleeping with Bread: Holding What Gives You Life*. Mahwah, NJ: Paulist Press, page 25.

25. www.ignatianspirituality.com/ignatian-prayer/the-examen

26. Kabat-Zinn, J. (2012). *Mindfulness for Life: An Interview with Jon Kabat-Zinn*. DVD. Mill Valley, CA: Psychotherapy.net.

Mindfulness and Christian Character

1. Peterson, C. & Seligman, M. E. P. (2004). *Character Strengths and Virtues: A Handbook and Classification*. Oxford: Oxford University Press.

2. More information at www.viacharacter.org

3. Full details available for download at www.viacharacter.org/www/Character-Strengths/VIA-Classification

4. Niemiec, R. M. (2013). VIA character strengths: Research and practice (the first 10 years). In H. H. Knoop & A. Delle Fave (eds.), *Well-being and Cultures: Perspectives on Positive Psychology*. New York: Springer, pages 11–30.

5. McGrath, R. E. (2015). Character strengths in 75 nations: An update. *The Journal of Positive Psychology*, 10(1), pages 41–52.

6. Sundararajan, L. (2005). Happiness donut: A Confucian critique of positive psychology. *Journal of Theoretical and Philosophical Psychology*, 25(1), pages 35–60.

7. Lewis, C. S. (1947). *The Abolition of Man: How Education Develops Man's Sense of Morality*. New York: Macmillan.

8. Niemiec, R. M. (2014). *Mindfulness and Character Strengths: A Practical Guide to Flourishing*. Boston, MA: Hogrefe.

9. Niemiec, R. M., Rashid, T. & Spinella, M. (2012). Strong mindfulness: Integrating mindfulness and character strengths. *Journal of Mental Health Counseling*, 34(3), pages 240–253.

10. Baumeister, R. F., Bratslavsky, E., Finkenauer, C. & Vohs, K. D. (2001). Bad is stronger than good. *Review of General Psychology*, 5(4), pages 323–370.

11. Lewis, S. (2011). *Positive Psychology at Work: How Positive Leadership and Appreciative Inquiry Create Inspiring Organizations*. Chichester: Wiley-Blackwell.

12. Thorne, B. (2003). *Infinitely Beloved*. London: Darton, Longman & Todd.

Mindful Gratitude

1. Explained in Linehan, M. M. (1993b). *Skills Training Manual for Treating Borderline Personality Disorder*. New York: Guilford Press.

2. Steindl-Rast, D. (2004). Gratitude as thankfulness and as gratefulness. In R. A. Emmons (ed.), *The Psychology of Gratitude*. New York, NY: Oxford University Press, pages 282–289.

3. For more details of Bob Emmons' work see Emmons, R. A. & McCullough, M. E. (eds.). (2004). *The Psychology of Gratitude*. Oxford: Oxford University

Press; and Emmons, R. A. (2007). *Thanks!: How the New Science of Gratitude Can Make You Happier.* New York: Houghton Mifflin.

4. Seligman, M. E. P., Steen, T. A., Park, N. & Peterson, C. (2005). Positive psychology progress: Empirical validation of interventions. *American Psychologist,* 60(5), pages 410–421.

5. See for example, Sheldon, K. M. & Lyubomirsky, S. (2012). The challenge of staying happier: Testing the hedonic adaptation prevention model. *Personality & Social Psychology Bulletin,* 38(5), pages 670–680.

6. e.g. Emmons, R. A. & McCullough, M. E. (2003). Counting blessings versus burdens: An experimental investigation of gratitude and subjective well-being in daily life. *Journal of Personality and Social Psychology,* 84(2), pages 377–389.

7. Referred to in, Sheldon, K. M. & Lyubomirsky, S. (2006). How to increase and sustain positive emotion: The effects of expressing gratitude and visualizing best possible selves. *The Journal of Positive Psychology,* 1(2), pages 73–82.

8. Heidegger, M. (1968). *What is Called Thinking?* (J. G. Gray, tr.). London: HarperColllins.

9. Nouwen, H. (1992). *The Return of the Prodigal Son.* London: Darton, Longman & Todd.

Mindful Wisdom

1. Bonhoeffer, D. (1986), *Ethics.* (E. Bethge, ed.). New York: Macmillan, pages 68–69.

2. Sternberg, R. J., Reznitskaya, A. & Jarvin, L. (2007). Teaching for wisdom: What matters is not just what students know, but how they use it. *London Review of Education,* 5(2), pages 143–158.

3. Baltes, P. B. & Staudinger, U. M. (2000). Wisdom: A metaheuristic (pragmatic) to orchestrate mind and virtue toward excellence. *American Psychologist,* 55(1), pages 122–136.

4. Wink, P. & Helson, R. (1997). Practical and transcendent wisdom: Their nature and some longitudinal findings. *Journal of Adult Development*, 4(1), pages 1–15.

5. For a review see Wong, P. T. P. (ed.). (2012). *The Human Quest for Meaning* (2nd ed.). New York: Routledge.

6. Compare, for example, the hope theories of Snyder, C. R. (1994). *The Psychology of Hope: You Can Get There from Here*. New York: Free Press; and Scioli, A. & Biller, H. B. (2009). *Hope in the Age of Anxiety*. Oxford: Oxford University Press.

7. This is largely due to the role of mindfulness in increasing emotional regulation, for an example see: Arch, J. J. & Craske, M. G. (2006). Mechanisms of mindfulness: Emotion regulation following a focused breathing induction. *Behaviour Research and Therapy*, 44(12), pages 1849–1858.

8. Marsha Linehan explains this approach to wise mind in Linehan, M. M. (1993a). *Cognitive-behavioral Treatment of Borderline Personality Disorder*. New York: Guilford Press.

9. For the use of perspective as a synonym for wisdom see www.viacharacter.org/www/Character-Strengths/VIA-Classification

10. Collicutt, J. (2015). *The Psychology of Christian Character Formation*. London: SCM, page 82.

11. The wise person exercise is included in Rashid, T. & Ajum, A. (2014). *Ways to Use VIA Character Strengths*. Retrieved from www.viacharacter.org/resources/ways-to-use-via-character-strengths/

The Mindful Organization

1. See for example, Hülsheger, U. R., Alberts, H. J. E. M., Feinholdt, A. & Lang, J. W. B. (2013). Benefits of mindfulness at work: The role of mindfulness in emotion regulation, emotional exhaustion, and job satisfaction. *Journal of Applied Psychology*, 98(2), pages 310–325.

2. See for example, www.workstress.net/sites/default/files/clearwater-2010-project.doc

3. Guidance on workplace stress legislation can be accessed from ACAS at, www.acas.org.uk/media/pdf/l/m/B18_1.pdf

4. Bunting, M. (2011). *Willing Slaves: How the Overwork Culture is Ruling Our Lives.* London: HarperCollins UK.

5. Ibid.

6. Greenleaf, R. K. (1998). *The Power of Servant Leadership.* San Francisco, CA: Berrett-Koehler.

7. For example, see Wright, T. A. (2013). More than meets the eye: The role of employee well-being in organizational research. In P. A. Linley, S. Harrington & N. Garcea (eds.), *The Oxford Handbook of Positive Psychology and Work.* New York: Oxford University Press, pages 143–154.

8. Robertson, I. T., Cooper, C. L., Sarkar, M. & Curran, T. (2015). Resilience training in the workplace from 2003 to 2014: A systematic review. *Journal of Occupational and Organizational Psychology,* 88(3), pages 533–562.

9. Alidina, S. & Adams, J. (2014). *Mindfulness at Work for Dummies.* Chichester: John Wiley & Sons.

10. For example, Aikens, K. A., Astin, J., Pelletier, K. R., Levanovich, K., Baase, C. M., Park, Y. Y. & Bodnar, C. M. (2014). Mindfulness goes to work: Impact of an online workplace intervention. *Journal of Occupational and Environmental Medicine,* 56(7), pages 721–731.

11. Bunting, M. (2011).

12. See Baltes, B. B., Clarke, M. A. & Chakrabarti, M. (2013). Work-life balance: The roles of work-family conflict and work-family facilitation. In P. A. Linley, S. Harrington & N. Garcea (eds.), *The Oxford Handbook of Positive Psychology and Work.* New York: Oxford University Press, pages 201–212.

13. Collins, J. C. (2001a). Level 5 leadership: The triumph of humility and fierce resolve. *Harvard Business Review,* January, pages 66–76.

14. Collins, J. C. (2001b). *Good to Great.* New York: Random House Business.

15. Collins (2001a), page 73.

16. Greenleaf (1998).

17. Ou, A. Y., Tsui, A. S., Kinicki, A. J., Waldman, D. A., Xiao, Z. & Song, L. J. (2014). Humble chief executive officers' connections to top management team integration and middle managers' responses. *Administrative Science Quarterly,* 59(1), pages 34–72.

18. Owens, B. P., Johnson, M. D. & Mitchell, T. R. (2013). Expressed humility in organizations: Implications for performance, teams, and leadership. *Organization Science,* 24(5), pages 1517–1538.

19. For example this link is made in, Kabat-Zinn, J. (2003). Mindfulness-based interventions in context: Past, present, and future. *Clinical Psychology: Science and Practice,* 10(2), pages 144–156.

20. Chancellor, J. & Lyubomirsky, S. (2013). Humble beginnings: Current trends, state perspectives, and hallmarks of humility. *Social and Personality Psychology Compass,* 7(11), pages 819–833.

21. Ross, L. D. (1977). The intuitive psychologist and his shortcomings: Distortions in the attribution process. In L. Berkowitz (ed.), *Advances in Experimental Social Psychology* (Vol. 10). New York: Academic Press, pages 174–221.

22. Philippians 4:2–3.

23. Jamison, C. (2006). *Finding Sanctuary: Monastic Steps for Everyday Life.* London: Liturgical Press.